PSYCHOSOMATIC

· · · · · · · · E L I Z A B E T H A . W I L S O N

· · · · · · · · · # PSYCHOSOMATIC

· · · · · · · · Feminism and the Neurological Body

Duke University Press   Durham / London 2004

© 2004 Duke University Press   All rights reserved
Printed in the United States of America on acid-free paper ∞
Typeset in Minion by Keystone Typesetting, Inc.
Library of Congress Cataloging-in-Publication data
appear on the last printed page of this book.

Instead of talking about the natural and the unnatural—or even nature and culture—we can talk about the parts of nature we prefer and why we prefer them.—Adam Phillips, *Darwin's Worms*

CONTENTS

• • • • • • • •   A C K N O W L E D G M E N T S

• • • • • • • •

• • • • • • • •   This book was written under the auspices of an Austra-
lian Research Council Postdoctoral Fellowship, held in the Research Institute for Humanities and Social Sciences (RIHSS) at the University of
Sydney. My thanks to Paul Patton, Margaret Harris, Rowanne Couch, and
Melissa McMahon for their support at RIHSS. It has been an exemplary
research environment, and a happy place to work.
    Sydney continues to give me wonderful intellectual allies, especially Helen
Keane, Vicki Kirby, Elizabeth McMahon, Robert Reynolds, and Vanessa
Smith. Peta Allen Shera did great research work for me. During the writing
of this book I was a member of the Silvan Tomkins Research Group in Syd-
ney; I have learned many good things in the company of Maria Angel, Susan
Best, Anna Gibbs, Melissa Hardie, Doris McIlwain, and Gillian Straker.
Isobel Pegrum has been the most wonderful friend, and Jeanette Martin has
made all the good things better.
    In the United States and the United Kingdom I am grateful to Karen
Barad, Penelope Deutscher, Richard Doyle, Anne Fausto-Sterling, Michael
Fortun, Mariam Fraser, Marsha Rosengarten, Susan Squier, and Elizabeth
Weed, who have responded to my work generously and have invited me into
their workplaces and oftentimes their homes. They have made my intellectual world richer and more emotionally substantial. Much of the material in
this book was test-driven at the annual conferences of the Society for Literature and Science. The SLS has been an important source of intellectual
encouragement for me over many years; many thanks to my colleagues and
friends at SLS for their hospitality. Reynolds Smith at Duke University Press

has been generous in his editorial support; his persistence and good humor have given a clarity to the book that I could not have produced on my own.

Versions of some chapters have been published previously. The introduction first appeared as "Somatic Compliance—Feminism, Biology and Science," *Australian Feminist Studies* 14(29): 7–18; a revised version is reprinted here with the permission of the journal. Chapter 1 first appeared as "Melancholic Biology: Prozac, Freud, and Neurological Determinism," *Configurations* 7: 403–419; a revised version is reprinted here with the permission of Johns Hopkins University Press. Chapter 3 first appeared as "Neurological Preference: LeVay's Study of Sexual Orientation," *SubStance* 91 29(1): 23–38; a revised version is reprinted here with the permission of the University of Wisconsin Press. Chapter 4 first appeared as "Darwin's Nervous System: Investigating Critical and Physiological Psychologies," *Australian Psychologist* 36(1): 62–69; a revised version is reprinted here with the permission of the Australian Psychological Society.

· · · · · · · · · INTRODUCTION

· · · · · · · · Somatic Compliance

· · · · · · · ·   In a letter to Sigmund Freud on September 17, 1924, Karl Abraham reports that he has just purchased from an antiquarian catalogue a paper written by Freud forty-six years earlier. The paper is Freud's third publication, and it is on the nervous system of the lamprey (Freud 1878). Politely negotiating his antiquarian status, Freud replies: "It is making severe demands on the unity of the personality to try to make me identify myself with the author of the paper on the spinal ganglia of the petromyzon. Nevertheless, it does seem to be the case, and I think I was happier about that discovery than about others since then" (2002, 515).

It has been usual to locate the beginnings of psychoanalysis in Freud's clinical encounters with hysterical patients in the 1880s and 1890s. It was from the strange aggregations of psyche and soma—paralyses, amnesias, strangulated affects, nervous tics, and infantile fantasies—that Freud was able to forge the foundations of psychoanalytic theory and method. This approach to reading Freud has stressed the importance of the body for psychoanalysis. A strong case has been made, via hysteria, that the psychological tenets of psychoanalysis are indebted to somatic symptomology—that the psyche is always already of the body.

Yet perhaps the body in psychoanalysis has been understood in terms that are too narrow. There has been a tendency, especially in feminist writing, to disregard Freud's neuroscientific and prepsychoanalytic bodies. I would like to extend the somatic beginnings of psychoanalysis back further than hysteria—further chronologically, further phylogenetically. Psychoanalysis can be approached, I argue, not just through the hysterized body of the patient, but also through the spinal ganglia of the petromyzon.

Before shifting to a medical career in the early 1880s (a shift that threw him into contact with his hysterical coconspirators Fliess, Charcot, and Dora), Freud spent six years working as a scientific researcher in the physiological laboratory at the University of Vienna under the supervision of Professor Ernst Brücke (Bernfield 1949, 1951; Freud 1925a). Freud's first research project in this lab was an investigation of the spinal cord in the lamprey. The lamprey (petromyzon) is a primitive fish that lacks a jaw and cartilaginous skeleton and has a sucker mouth; it is eel-like in appearance, having scaleless, slimy skin. One outcome of Freud's research was the demonstration of morphological continuities—at the cellular level—between the lamprey and the higher fishes. What differentiated primitive and advanced nervous systems, Freud concluded, was not the cellular elements per se, but the manner of their organization.

Oliver Sacks (1998b) comments on the evolutionary implications of this connection between the lower and the higher: "There emerged, even in Freud's earliest researches, a sense of a Darwinian evolution whereby, using the most conservative means (i.e., the same basic anatomic cellular elements), more and more complex nervous systems could be built" (222). Freud's histological investigation, then, isn't limited to the lowly body of the lamprey. His data touch on other (higher) fish and implicate all vertebrate nervous systems. As Bernfield (1949) argues, even psychological questions are put into play by Freud's paper on the spinal ganglia: "Together with the problem of the structure of the nervous elements goes the interesting question of whether the nervous system of the higher animals, at least of the vertebratae, is composed of elements different from the nervous system of the lower animals; or whether the simple and the complicated systems alike are built of the same units . . . Are the differences in the mind of higher and lower animals only a matter of degree of complication? Does the human mind differ from that of some mollusce?" (176).

Freud says to Abraham that the lamprey and the body of work it generated place severe demands on the unity of his character forty years later. James Strachey surmises that around the time of this interchange with Abraham, Freud was writing "The Resistances to Psychoanalysis" (1925c).[1] In this paper Freud dates the beginning of psychoanalysis, not from the lamprey, but from his contact with Breuer, Charcot, and hypnosis. Moreover, he chastises his physician colleagues for their neglect of psychogenic factors in the etiology of hysteria and their preference for "anatomical, physical and chemical factors" (215). In 1924 Freud saw anatomy, physiology, and chemistry as demands on—resistances to—psychoanalysis. On Freud's receipt of Abraham's letter, the nervous system of the lamprey could not have been further from his mind.[2]

Nonetheless, the demands of the fish's body do not diminish the farther either Freud or we move away from the physiological laboratory in the 1870s. The tiny splinters of this body can be found throughout Freud's work and throughout everything that has touched or refused psychoanalysis since.[3] These fragments carry within them the full force of the demand Freud felt pressing on his own personal integrity in 1924, and they push with no less urgency at the coherence of contemporary accounts of embodiment and materiality. The lamprey places two demands on our current-day analyses of the body: biology and reductionism. For many feminists, these amount to the same thing: biology is reductive materiality stripped of the animating effects of culture and sociality. In a theoretical scene that is bent instinctively toward correcting, reversing, or resisting the forces of biological reductionism, the body of Freud's fish has been rendered unintelligible. Its biologism and its reductionism are articulate only in their capacity to signal that complexity is to be found elsewhere or later on. The cold, dead body of the lamprey is taken to be a benchmark against which not only Freud's theoretical progress, but also our own critical sophistication can be measured.

It appears to me, however, that this consignment of the fish to the past—its relegation to what has preceded us historically and analytically—is itself a gesture of reductionism. It is to presuppose that the nervous system of the lamprey doesn't communicate past the dissection table, or past 1878. In this book I explore how some biologically reductionist demands have the potential to expand our theories of the body in important, innovative, and sometimes exhilarating ways. My first hypothesis is this: Those moments when Freud relies most heavily on biological or reductionist declarations are not necessarily the moments when his accounts become static, incoherent, or critically useless. In fact, these moments of biological reduction often produce Freud's most acute formulations about the nature of the body and the character of the psyche. This hypothesis about the value of simple biological events is one that I test in this book in relation to the neurological theories of—not only Freud—but also Charles Darwin, Oliver Sacks, Simon LeVay, Paul MacLean, and Joseph LeDoux.

What new accounts of the body are possible if we are able to keep the body of the lamprey in mind? What new modes of embodiment become legible when biological reductionism is tolerated and explored? Let me return to the more familiar ground of hysteria (and feminism) to offer a reformulation of the nervous body in terms of biology and reductionism.

A Curious Hysterical Symptom

The hysterical body has been an exemplary point of reference for feminist accounts of the corporeal. The nineteenth-century hysterical body was employed extensively in early feminist discussions of the body and its relation to culture.[4] In its strange contemporary forms (eating disorders, chronic fatigue syndrome, group mourning, psychosomatic epidemics), hysteria continues to challenge any presumption that we now know the body and have grasped its capacities and limitations. Despite the wide variety of feminist methodologies that have no direct association with psychoanalysis, the phenomenon of hysteria—the corporeal revelation of psychic and cultural conflict—retains its hold on our political and critical imagination.

However, it is not just hysteria in general that has been of interest to feminist theorists of the body. Of the different forms that hysteria could take (e.g., anxiety hysteria, hysteroepilepsy), it was one particular configuration that seemed to illustrate feminist concerns with greatest force: conversion hysteria. Paralyses, facial neuralgias, loss of vision or voice, tics, bodily pains, and chronic muscular contractions were common symptoms of nineteenth-century conversion hysteria. Joseph Breuer and Sigmund Freud's early writings (Breuer and Freud 1895) were particularly influential in inciting feminist interest in hysterical symptomology. By arguing that conversion hysterics were suffering from repressed ideas and strangulated affects rather than degeneracy, Breuer and Freud gave an account of psychosomatic pathology that was immensely productive for feminist accounts of the corporeal. Their most famous conversion hysterics, Anna O. and Dora, became exemplary figures of embodied insubordination (Appignanesi and Forrester 1992; Bernheimer and Kahane 1990).

Nonetheless, at the same time that conversion hysteria came to stand in for all hysteria, there was a narrowing of the character of conversion hysteria itself. Specifically, there was a foreclosure on the biology of conversion hysteria in most feminist expositions; the particularities of the muscles, nerves, and organs in their hysterical state have remained underexamined and some of the more remarkable questions about hysteria remain unasked. Take, for example, the cases of conversion hysteria documented by Breuer and Freud. After the death of her father, Anna O. suffered from an acute hysterical attack during which "there was a high degree of restriction of the field of vision: in a bunch of flowers which gave her much pleasure she could only see one flower at a time. She complained of not being able to recognise people" (1895, 26). Miss Lucy R.'s lost sense of smell was restored when she recounted two forgotten traumas associated with her employer. Frau Emmy von N.'s hysterical gastric pains were relieved by Freud's stroking her "a few times across the epigastrium" (64). By and large, the bio-logic of these transformations has been overlooked in feminist commentary on hysteria. After all, what is the neurology of a transitory visual agnosia? By what physiological means can memory restore the sense of smell? What biological mechanisms are in play when gastric pains are removed by the placement of the analyst's hands on the patient's abdomen? The biology of these symptoms is complicated further by the fact that somatic conversion is usually the effect of deferred action (*Nachträglichkeit*). Symptoms emerge only after a delay; an originary trauma is usually insufficient to initiate symptoms of conversion. The biology of hysteria encompasses not simply the logic of spatiality (Which body part?) but also the logic of temporality (At what time? In what order?).

Following Breuer and Freud, feminists have tended to retreat from the biology of hysteria and theorize hysteria as primarily ideational. It has been almost universally agreed among feminist commentators that what is most interesting politically and what is most important theoretically in hysteria is the complex condensation and displacement of ideational content that motivates hysterical attacks. The way these contorted ideational structures are then converted into bodily symptoms has attracted less attention than one might expect. Oddly enough, it is the very mechanism of conversion (of psyche into soma) that has been the least explored aspect of conversion hysteria. We may be well equipped to answer why hysterics convert, but we appear to be collectively mute in response to the question of how they convert.[5] Breuer and Freud's oft-quoted axiom that "hysterics suffer mainly from reminiscences" (1895, 7) has been deployed perhaps too partially. Hysterics do indeed suffer from reminiscences; they also suffer from bodily symptoms: they are paralyzed, blinded, in physical pain, they cough incessantly, they have difficulty breathing. Perhaps the most obvious aspect of hysteria—the bodily disability—has been attenuated in feminist accounts of hysterical symptomology.

The preference for analyses of ideational contortion at the expense of analyses of biological conversion suggests that the question of the body has yet to be posed as comprehensively as it could be. It seems to me that the neurology, physiology, or biochemistry of hysterical symptomology can be disregarded only in a theoretical milieu that takes biology to be inert, a milieu that, despite its expressed interest in rethinking the body, still presumes that the microstructure of the body does not contribute to the play of condensation, displacement, and deferred action that is now so routinely attributed to culture, signification, or sociality. Though the body may be the locale of these intricate operations, biology itself is rarely considered to be a source of such accomplishment.

Elaine Showalter's (1985) account of hysteria exemplifies this tendency and demonstrates the manner in which a retreat from biology became naturalized early in the feminist interest in hysteria.[6] Showalter gives a short account of one of Jean-Martin Charcot's most famous hysterics, Augustine, who entered Charcot's ward in the Salpêtrière at the age of fifteen. Augustine adapted quickly and with some enthusiasm to Charcot's practice of photographing his patients when they were in the grip of an acute hysterical attack. The photographs of Augustine in various poses of hysterical rapture are perhaps the most widely disseminated and recognized illustrations of nineteenth-century hysteria (Copjec 1987; Didi-Huberman 1982). Showalter describes Augustine's behavior and its consequences thus:

> Among [Augustine's] gifts was her ability to time and divide her hysterical performances into scenes, acts, tableaux, and intermissions, to perform on cue and on schedule with the click of a camera.
>
> But Augustine's cheerful willingness to assume whatever poses her audience desired took its toll on her psyche. During the period when she was being repeatedly photographed, she developed a curious hysterical symptom: she began to see everything in black and white. (1985, 154)

A curious symptom indeed. However, in her rush to convey her distaste for Charcot's spectacular medicine, Showalter does not so much as pause to consider the biological extraordinariness of such a conversion. She continues immediately: "In 1880, [Augustine] began to rebel against the hospital regime; she had periods of violence in which she tore her clothes and broke windows. During these angry outbreaks she was anaesthetized with ether or chloroform. In June of that year, the doctors gave up their efforts with her case, and she was put in a locked cell" (154).

While her complaint is that Charcot took insufficient notice of the hysterics under his care, that they were simply specimens in his living museum of pathology, Showalter herself does not consider the detail of Augustine's affliction either. Showalter's vignette is no less immersed in sensationalism, no more turned to attentiveness of the patient, than are Charcot's staged images. If Charcot has reduced Augustine to being the very embodiment of hysteria, Showalter has confined her within a one-dimensional narrative of victimization (photographed, anaesthetized, locked up). Not only is the meaning of Augustine's visual symptomology deemed straightforward by Showalter (seemingly, Augustine's tragic capitulation to Charcot's psycho-photographic regime), but the very mechanism of this optical conversion passes without comment. What kind of biological material (retina, optic nerve, visual cortex) stops processing color under the sway of a photographic seduction? Why is the astonishment of Augustine's symptom attributed only to Charcot and not also to the remarkable, hysterical vicissitudes of Augustine's eyes and brain?[7] Surely, one of the most curious things about Augustine's symptom is that the nervous system is able to function according to "scenes, acts, tableaux, and intermissions, to perform on cue and on schedule with the click of a camera."

Around the same time, Monique David-Ménard (1989) offered a much more sophisticated account of hysteria and the body, an account in which the bodily symptoms of conversion are intimately tied to desire. She argues against a conventional psychosomatic explanation of conversion hysteria, wherein the organic body is said to be subjected to psychological incursions (representations, ideas, memories) that render it unwell. The difficulty with this kind of explanation is that it operates with two distinct, interacting categories: mind and body. No matter how intricately we explain hysterical symptoms as the interaction of the psychological and physiological, we still presume an ontological separation that David-Ménard finds conceptually intolerable and clinically inadequate. This psychosomatic model of conversion hysteria is evident early on in Freud's writing; however, it is soon replaced by a more accomplished theory in which the erotogenicity of the body is central: "Later he found a better way of identifying the body in question by saying that hysterical symptoms and crises constitute a pantomime of sexual pleasure" (3). For David-Ménard, the hysterical body prompts us to think in other than purely psychological or physiological categories: her analysis "brings to light a different order of reality, one that escapes the psychical-physiological alternative and that we shall designate as the order of pleasure-body" (28).

David-Ménard's elucidation of the pleasure-body and hysteria is astute. In many ways, her analysis of Freud's case of Fraulein Elisabeth eclipses the comments I offer below on this early analysis of conversion hysteria. Yet at the same time, David-Ménard enacts the same gestures I outlined above in relation to Showalter: more explicitly than Showalter, she shuns the biological. In the very first pages, David-Ménard declares of hysteria that it "is not acquainted with the anatomy of the nervous system" (2) and that "the physiological body is not what is involved" (3). As we know, hysterical symptoms do not follow the conventional logic of anatomy; an arm, for example, is paralyzed not according to biomedical maps of muscles and ligaments, but according to the logic of how an arm is usually dressed and used. But how has this differential enactment of anatomy become a repudiation of anatomy in general? How can a neurosis not be acquainted with the nervous system?

Vicki Kirby (1997) offers a compelling anecdote that demonstrates not only how readily biology is denounced in the name of feminism, but also how that denunciation has been central to the intelligibility of more sophisticated accounts of the body. Kirby attended a feminist philosophy conference at the height of the concern about essentialism, especially as it might emanate from the so-called French feminists. In a manner similar to David-Ménard's, a speaker on Irigaray takes great care to stress the figurative, libidinal, and evocative nature of Irigarayan embodiment over and above any naïve anatomical or biological concerns. This maneuver troubles Kirby:

If the audience was meant to be reassured by these remarks, requiring this explanatory caveat before the paper could be taken seriously, I was left wondering what danger had been averted by the exclusion of biology . . . When I asked a question to this effect, it was met with a certain nervous incomprehension. Deciding, perhaps, that I must still be immersed in a precritical understanding of the body, the speaker dismissed me with a revealing theatrical gesture. As if to emphasize the sheer absurdity of my question she pinched herself and commented, "Well, I certainly don't mean *this* body." And so it seemed that with a gesture so matter of fact that it required no further comment, the fact of (the) matter was both decided and dispatched. (70)

By passing over neurophysiology, Showalter and David-Ménard miss some of the most compelling questions about conversion hysteria, and, regrettably, they imply that biological data lie beyond the confines of feminist analysis. Showalter's description of Augustine's hysteria renders the retina, the optic nerve, and the brain psychologically inert and politically barren, mere ciphers for a complexity that is located elsewhere. Similarly, David-Ménard has moved as quickly and naturally as the speaker in Kirby's anecdote to declare that the neurophysiological body is soma non grata to a sophisticated account of hysteria.

The analyses that follow in this book are my attempt to slow down the speed with which renunciations of the biological can happen in feminist writing on the body. I have taken the nervous system as my test case. This preference for neurological analysis does not imply that cultural, social, linguistic, literary, or historical analyses are somehow secondary considerations. Rather, my point is that the cultural, social, linguistic, literary, and historical analyses that now dominate the scene of feminist theory typically seek to seal themselves off from—or constitute themselves against—the domain of the biological. Curiously enough, feminist theories of the body are often exemplary in this regard. Despite the intensive scrutiny of the body in feminist theory and in the humanities in general over the past two decades, certain fundamental aspects of the body, biology, and materiality have been foreclosed. After all, how many feminist accounts of the anorexic body pay serious attention to the biological functions of the stomach, the mouth, or the digestive system? How many feminist analyses of the anxious body are informed and illuminated by neurological data? How many feminist discussions of the sexual body have been articulated through biochemistry? It is my argument that biology—the muscular capacities of the body, the function of the internal organs, the biophysics of cellular metabolism, the microphysiology of circulation, respiration, digestion, and excretion—needs to become a more significant contributor to feminist theories of the body.

The Case of Fraulein Elisabeth von R.

Fraulein Elisabeth was a young woman who came to Freud with constant pains in her legs that left her unable to walk, stand, or even lie down with any comfort at all. Freud describes her symptoms thus:

> The pain was of an indefinite character; I gathered that it was something in the nature of a painful fatigue. A fairly large, ill-defined area of the anterior surface of the right thigh was indicated as the focus of the pains, from which they most often radiated and where they reached their greatest intensity. In this area the skin and muscles were also particularly sensitive to pressure and pinching . . . This hyperalgesia of the skin and muscles was not restricted to this area but could be observed more or less over the whole of both legs. The muscles were perhaps even more sensitive to pain than the skin; but there could be no question that the thighs were the parts most sensitive to both these kinds of pain. (Breuer and Freud 1895, 135–136)

Freud's analysis of Fraulein Elisabeth—his first full analysis—uncovers a series of distressing moments that facilitated these physical pains. Fraulein Elisabeth's father had been bedridden for many months with an illness that would eventually kill him. During this time Fraulein Elisabeth devoted herself to nursing and caring for him, at the expense of pursuing an attachment to a potential lover. The site of the hysterical pain in her right leg was revealed to be the place where her ill father would rest his foot every morning as Fraulein Elisabeth changed the bandages on his leg. The pains in her left leg were traced to an unacknowledged love for her sister's husband, a love complicated by Fraulein Elisabeth's great attachment to her sister. The death of the sister provoked Fraulein Elisabeth to consider—while standing at the sister's deathbed, no less—that the beloved husband was now free and she could become his wife.

I want to leave to one side a discussion of the psychological mechanisms that triggered these particular pains. The conflicts between familial devotion and erotic desire are, surely, already familiar enough. What strikes me as more pertinent in this case history, and less familiar to a contemporary feminist audience, is the biology of Fraulein Elisabeth's conversion. What are the physiological mechanisms that allow the thigh muscles to function differently: the right thigh muscle in response to her father, and the left thigh muscle in response to her brother-in-law? What is in the nature of the muscles that makes them so psychologically attuned? Freud offers little help on the physiological mechanisms of bodily conversion: "I cannot, I must confess, give any hint of how a conversion of this kind is brought about. It is obviously not carried out in the same way as an intentional and voluntary action. It is a process which occurs under the pressure of the motive of defence in someone whose organization—or a temporary modification of it—has a proclivity in that direction" (Breuer and Freud 1895, 166).

Importantly, Freud doesn't take refuge in the central nervous system. It is not to the brain or the higher cortical surfaces that he looks for an explanation of conversion. It is as though he suspects that the psychic conflicts have been devolved to the lower body parts: here, psychic defense is more muscular than it is cerebral. The muscle fibers, nerves, blood vessels of the left leg, and the muscle fibers, nerves, blood vessels of the right leg have become functionally differentiated under the influence of a psychic defense that isn't necessarily centralized in the brain and that certainly isn't contained within Fraulein Elisabeth herself. That is, Fraulein Elisabeth's leg muscles are not merely expressing her own internal psychic conflicts, they are also in dialogue with others: her father, her sister, her brother-in-law, and, not least of all, Freud.[8] On this latter point, Freud presents a striking clinical note:

> Her painful legs began to "join in the conversation" during our analyses. What I have in mind is the following remarkable fact. As a rule the patient was free from pain when we started work. If, then, by a question or by pressure upon her head I called up a memory, a sensation of pain would make its first appearance, and this was usually so sharp that the patient would give a start and put her hand to the painful spot. The pain that was thus aroused would persist so long as she was under the influence of the memory; it would reach its climax when she was in the act of telling me the essential and decisive part of what she had to communicate, and with the last word of this it would disappear. I came in time to use such pains as a compass to guide me; if she stopped talking but admitted that she still had a pain, I knew that she had not told me everything, and insisted on her continuing her story till the pain had been talked away. (148)

The real force of Fraulein Elisabeth's condition is that the physiology of her thigh muscles (their capacity to stretch and contract; their intimacy with the peripheral nervous system) cannot be separated from the illness and death of her father or from the words of her analyst. The intersubjectivity of her analysis is facilitated not just by words, ideation, and affects but also by nerves, blood vessels, and skin. The conversation between Fraulein Elisabeth and Freud is verbal, interpersonal, and biological. The hystericization of Fraulein Elisabeth's thighs is just one particular configuration of complicity (muscles-memories) in a field that is nothing but such intersubjective, biologically attuned complicities (. . . muscles-skin-legs-father-sister-hands-words-pain-analyst . . .). Consider the remarkable occurrence of Fraulein Elisabeth's continuing her story until the pains had been talked away. The familiar retort that such pains are all in her head seems to explain nothing; it restates rather than dissects the puzzle. Yet, taken literally (reductively), it perhaps gets us closer to the heart of the matter. If the pains are indeed all in her head, then this entails a number of reciprocal ontological contortions: that her thigh is her head, that her mind is muscular, and that Freud's words are in the nature of her nervous system.[9]

Biological Proclivities

For Freud, hysterical conversion is "a process which occurs . . . in someone whose [biological] organization . . . has a proclivity in that direction" (Breuer and Freud 1895, 166). In his best-known case of conversion hysteria, the case of Dora, Freud (1905) gives the name "somatic compliance" to this proclivity. In cases of conversion hysteria, a preexisting organic condition facilitates the production of symptoms (that is, hysterical symptoms are not biologically arbitrary). This facilitation may be either hereditary or contingent in nature; Fraulein Elisabeth, for example, exhausted herself both emotionally and physically by taking a long walk in the mountains with her adored brother-in-law, thus facilitating the compliance of her legs to her inchoate hysteria.

While insisting in the Dora case that hysterical symptoms require "the participation of *both* sides" (i.e., the somatic and the psychic; Freud 1905, 40), Freud affirms his own proclivity for psychological explanation: "For therapeutic purposes the most important determinants are those given by the fortuitous psychological material; the clearing-up of the symptoms is achieved by looking for their psychical significance" (41). As Freud turned more particularly to psychological explanation, the attention paid to the role of biology in hysteria was attenuated, and a more sustained theory of the soma's compliant nature was never undertaken. David-Ménard chose to move forward from these difficulties in order to discover the pleasure-body in Freud's later work; I need to return to his early, reductive writings to encounter the biology of hysterical conversion more fully. In 1894 Freud placed biology at the very heart of hysterical etiology: "The characteristic factor in hysteria is not splitting of consciousness but *the capacity for conversion*, and we may adduce as an important part of the disposition to hysteria—a disposition which in other respects is still unknown—a psycho-physical aptitude for transposing very large sums of excitation into the somatic innervation" (1899b, 50). Of course, this return to the biology of hysteria, to somatic compliance, or to a psychophysical aptitude for hysteria brings us uneasily close to nineteenth-century formulations of degeneracy; nonetheless, the centrality of biology to the etiology of psychopathology incites a proliferation of biological ontologies. Rather than disregarding

Freud at those moments when he invokes biology, we may be better served by a more careful consideration of the data he lays before us.

One important, perhaps formative event in Freud's early biological writings was the revelation of male hysteria. On his return from sabbatical at the Salpêtrière in 1886, Freud presented a theoretical paper to the Vienna Society of Medicine on male hysteria, one of the diagnostic discoveries for which Charcot had become infamous. The paper was not well received and Freud was challenged to procure a case of male hysteria that could be presented to the Society. His 1886 paper on hysterical hemianesthesia (loss of sensation on one side of the body) in a man documents this clinical presentation. Strachey notes that this case history predates the blossoming of Freud's psychological interests; it is concerned primarily with the physical characteristics of this patient's hysterical symptoms. Strachey's editorial comments imply that the empiricism of this case history—its focus on biological detail—holds only incidental interest for the psychoanalytically inclined reader.

Nonetheless, I would like to pause to consider these physical phenomena more closely. In presenting this case history, Freud provides a meticulous description of the man's physical incapacities. For example: "If we now proceed to an examination of the trunk and extremities, here again we find an absolute anesthesia, in the first place in the left arm. As you see, I can push a pointed needle through a fold of the skin without the patient reacting against it. The deep parts—muscles, ligaments, joints—must also be insensitive to an equally high degree, since I can twist the wrist-joint and stretch the ligaments without provoking any feeling in the patient" (1886, 28).

Freud's biological examination allows us to see the extensive reach of hysteria into this man's body. The patient's hemianesthesia extends through the whole of the left side of his body—hystericizing, for example, the muscles, ligaments, and joints of the left arm and leg, the visual function of the left eye, the gag reflex of the left side of the throat, and the left spermatic cord. Of necessity, explications of this kind bring the biology of hysteria into acute relief, and for feminists trained in cultural, social, or linguistic analysis there appears to be little here out of which a critical account of hysteria or corporeality could be forged. Freud's account seems too literal. However, if we avert our eyes too quickly from this scene, if we turn elsewhere to grasp the nature of these symptoms, we will miss what is most noteworthy here: a description of somatic compliance. This matter-of-fact description reveals the compliant and complicitous character of this man's body. The capacity of the mucous membranes of the throat to convert to anesthesia here, on the left, but not there, on the right, demonstrates that biology is more naturally eccentric, more intrinsically preternatural than we usually allow. Against the popular feminist preference for cultural or social explications of this man's condition, I would like to maintain the focus here, on this body: on the nerves, blood vessels, and muscles as Freud's needle pushes through a fold of the skin. In this scene, the strange convolutions of hysteria are held within the confines of biological detail. Rather than reducing the nature of hysteria, this confinement allows the reader to perceive in biology a complexity usually attributed only to nonbiological domains.

The revelation of hysterical symptoms in a male body is a definitive moment in psychoanalytic history. It authorized a generalized theory of neurotic conversion that corrected the conventional reduction of hysteria to the female body. With the discovery of male hysteria, hysteria was no longer tied to the uterus or to the female body: it was now one of the vicissitudes of human biology in general. The medical notion of hysteria as a wandering womb has long been considered a violence against the female body. However, before such an etiology is dismissed altogether, the question of organic wandering demands closer examination. The notion of a roaming uterus contains within it a sense of organic matter that disseminates, strays, and deviates from its proper place. Perhaps all biology wanders.[10] Formulated this way, hysterical diversion is not forced on the throat, legs, or eyes from the outside, it is already part of the natural repertoire of biological matter. A more sustained focus on the biology of hysteria would allow us to see that the proclivity to conversion (diversion, perversion) is native to biochemical, physiological, and nervous systems.

In this short account of hysteria, I have endeavored to highlight the uses of biological reductionism, especially in relation to the nervous system, for feminist accounts of the body. I have argued that it is important to keep the peripheral nervous system in mind when thinking about the nervous body; similarly, the nervous systems of animals might be useful for critically astute formulations of human bodies. Both of these propositions are explored further in the chapters that follow. Throughout the book, I am interested in the potential in the neurosciences for reinvention and transformation. For too long the neurosciences have been the target of feminist censure when they could be active, innovative contributors to feminist scholarship. In the past twenty years, feminists have produced pioneering theories of the body: they have demonstrated how bodies vary across different cultural contexts, how gender fabricates them in very precise ways, how they are being transformed by technological invention. However, these feminist theories have usually been reluctant to engage with biological data; they retain, and encourage, the fierce antibiologism that marked the emergence of second-wave feminism. Most feminist research on the body relies on theories of social construction; in defiance of biological models, this research explores how cultural, social, or linguistic constraints shape the kinds of bodies we have. This book takes a different approach: it contends that feminism can be deeply and happily complicit with biological explanation; it argues that feminist accounts of the body could be more affectionately involved with neurobiological data. The chapters that follow focus on psychopharmacology, neurogastroenterology, evolutionary theory, hypothalamic structures, reptilian temperament, and affective neuroscience. It is the presumption of this book that sustained interest in biological detail will have a reorganizing effect on feminist theories of the body—that exploring the entanglement of biochemistry, affectivity, and the physiology of the internal organs will provide us with new avenues into the body. Attention to neurological detail and a tolerance for reductive formulations will enable feminist research to move past its dependency on social constructionism and generate more vibrant, biologically attuned accounts of the body.

• • • • • • • • |

• • • • • • • •   Freud, Prozac, and Melancholic Neurology

• • • • • • • •   One of Peter Kramer's central case histories in his 1993 best-seller *Listening to Prozac* is the story of a young woman named Lucy. "Her history is dominated by one event. When Lucy was ten and living in a third-world country where her father was stationed, she came home to find her mother dead, shot by a young manservant—a beloved and trusted member of the household—who had become crazed and violent. Lucy showed no immediate reaction to this ghastly occurrence. She remained a productive, well-liked girl" (67).

As an adult, Lucy developed a heightened sensitivity to loss and rejection. She went to see Kramer to deal with this crippling oversensitivity. Her treatment with him involved both psychotherapy and the use of the SSRI (selective serotonin reuptake inhibitor) antidepressants Prozac and Zoloft.

In summarizing her case, Kramer draws attention to Lucy's biology: "Lucy had harbored a kernel of vulnerability that the psychotherapy did not touch. It was as if psychological trauma—the mother's death, and then the years of struggle for Lucy and her father—had produced physiological consequences for which the most direct remedy was a physiological intervention. But how does psychic trauma become translated into a functionally autonomous, biologically encoded personality trait? How can a mother's death become a change in serotonergic pathways?" (107).

This last question—How can a mother's death become a change in serotonergic pathways?—strikes me as pivotal, not simply to Kramer's project, but also to many contemporary critical and political discussions. In asking this question, Kramer invokes a series of long-familiar debates about the relation of psychology to biology. For many critics, his juxtaposition of a mother's death and serotonergic pathways indicates a dangerous tendency to neurological determinism; many of us suppose that we already know the answer to Kramer's question. Inevitably, we suspect, the complex psychological trauma of a mother's death will be brought under the sway of synapses, neurotransmitters, and cortical pathways, a process that Kramer himself names "the remarkable imperialism of the biological" (105).[1]

In this chapter I show how Kramer's hypotheses concerning the neuropsychology of depression lead in different directions, both biologically and analytically. I am interested in Kramer's interpretation of depression as a weakened neurological state. By juxtaposing *Listening to Prozac* with Freud's theories of neurasthenia (nervous weakness), I am able to examine the character of the neurology-psychology interface. Although the relations between neurology and psychology are unanimously declared to be complex, the exact nature of the interrelating components has been less carefully examined. Are they two discrete forces that enter into a complex, yet fundamentally straight relation? Or is their relationality somehow integral to their very nature? What relations of influence operate between such co-implicated domains?

Within the structures of neurological weakness that Kramer and Freud advocate, forces of influence and determination are more mutually entangled than the critics of neurological determinism have hitherto acknowledged. It is this that marks Kramer's and Freud's accounts as both distinctive and instructive. Extending the argument I began in the introduction, I maintain that close attention to neurological detail need not be at the expense of critical innovation or political efficacy. Kramer's and Freud's deployments of neurology are illuminating for a critical assessment of the neurosciences because they restage the now routine claims that neurological theories are always politically dangerous or imperialistic, that biology is a discursive ruse, or that the final word on any psychobiological event must always lie in the domain of social or cultural analysis. Importantly, this restaging is accomplished, not through the recitation of long familiar anti-determinist axioms, but through the iteration of reductive neurological hypotheses.

Nervous Weakness

Neurasthenia means "nervous weakness"; it is a disorder commonly associated with civilized culture at the end of the nineteenth century (Barke, Fribush, and Stearns 2000). Speaking clinically, neurasthenia is a debility of the nerves, causing fatigue, headaches, indigestion, constipation, listlessness, and impoverishment of sexual activity. The American physician George Beard coined the termed in 1869 (Gosling 1987). He wrote extensively about the nature of neurasthenic symptoms, attributing them to the moderniza-tion peculiar to American life in the late nineteenth century: "evil habits, excesses, tobacco, alcohol, worry and special excitements, even climate itself—all the familiar excitants being secondary to the one great predispos-ing cause—civilization" (Beard 1895, 15). Modern life was causing a chronic "feebleness and instability of nerve action," and this in turn produced in the individual an "excessive sensitiveness and irritability" (Beard in Goodall 1996, 65).

Beginning in the 1880s, Freud was also interested in neurasthenia, al-though he defined it much more narrowly than did Beard.[2] Freud claimed that neurasthenia is not due to excess of effort, overwork, or modernization. For Freud, neurasthenia is always and only a sexual neurosis.[3] Overwork and the stresses of modernization may trigger neurasthenia, but only where there is a preexisting nervous weakening caused by sexual dysfunction: "Sex-ual exhaustion can by itself alone provoke neurasthenia. If it fails to achieve this by itself, it has such an effect on the disposition of the nervous system that physical illness, depressive affects and overwork (toxic influences) can no longer be tolerated without [leading to] neurasthenia. Without sexual exhaustion, however, all these factors are incapable of generating neur-asthenia. They bring about normal fatigue, normal sorrow, normal physical weakness, but they only continue to give evidence of how much 'of these detrimental influences a normal person can tolerate' " (Freud 1893, 180).

Freud placed neurasthenia (along with hypochondria and anxiety neu-rosis) in the category of the actual neuroses—what might be called, these days, psychosomatic illness. The actual neuroses were distinguished in terms of their etiology from the psychoneuroses (hysteria, obsessional neurosis, melancholia, etc.). Freud argued that the causes of the actual neuroses were quite straightforward: they were to be found in the absence or the inade-quacy of sexual satisfaction. His classification of neurasthenia with the ac-tual neuroses allows us to note two things about its etiology:

1. Neurasthenia has its origin in the particularities of the patient's life as it is configured in the present, not in past infantile events or in repressed conflict. Thus, the "actual" of the phrase "actual neurosis" refers to actuality in the temporal sense of the here and now (Laplanche and Pontalis 1988). Specifically, it is immoderation in masturbation or the prolonged practice of coitus interruptus that Freud isolates as the behavioral determinants of neurasthenia. Or at least this is the case for men. In women, neurasthenia is rarely caused directly by masturbation, but more usually through inade-quate sexual relations with a neurasthenic husband: "Normally, girls are sound and not neurasthenic; and this is true as well of young married women, in spite of all the sexual traumas of this period of life. In com-paratively rare cases neurasthenia appears in married women and in older

unmarried ones in its pure form; it is then to be regarded as having risen spontaneously and in the same manner [? as in men]. Far more often neurasthenia in a married woman is derived from neurasthenia in a man or is produced simultaneously" (Freud 1893, 181). The transmission of neurasthenia from man to woman is not primarily psychological or cultural, but somatic. One sexually inadequate body generates another.

2. Neurasthenic symptoms are somatic or bodily rather than psychic in origin, and are not amenable to psychoanalytic intervention: "The essence of the theories about the 'actual neuroses' which I have put forward in the past and am defending to-day lies in my assertion, based on experiment, that their symptoms, unlike psychoneurotic ones, cannot be analyzed. That is to say, the constipation, headaches and fatigue of the so-called neurasthenic do not admit of being traced back historically or symbolically to operative experiences and cannot be understood as substitutes for sexual satisfaction or as compromises between opposing instinctual impulses, as is the case with psychoneurotic symptoms (even though the latter may perhaps have the same appearance)" (Freud 1912, 249). The mechanisms of symptom formation in neurasthenia are directly somatic; they are not psychic compromise formations but rather the "direct *somatic* consequences of sexual disturbances" (Freud 1916, 388). In this sense, "actual" refers to the unmediated nature of the symptom. There is no meaning to be uncovered and interpreted in either neurasthenia or anxiety neurosis; Freud believed that the actual neuroses were properly the concern of the biomedical sciences.[4]

Freud (1895b) offers an account of symptom formation in anxiety neurosis (one of the actual neuroses) in which these etiological notions are clearly articulated. In the sexually mature male, Freud suggests, somatic sexual excitation is produced almost constantly and eventually accumulates to a level where it impinges on the psyche. Specifically, it is "pressure on the walls of the seminal vesicles, which are lined with nerve endings," that eventually breaks through the resistance to the cerebral cortex and "express[es] itself as a psychical stimulus" (108). This cathects, or libidinizes, a series of sexual ideas in the psyche, producing a libidinal tension that demands to be discharged. The adequate discharge of this libidinal tension is possible only through "a complicated spinal reflex act which brings about the unloading of the nerve-endings, and in all the psychical preparations which have to be made in order to set off that reflex" (108). Freud calls this a specific or adequate action. That is, adequate discharge requires the synchronous release of somatic and psychic tension. Anything less than this will mean that accumulated somatic excitation will continue to breach the subcortical resistances and intrude into the psyche. A similar process is also attributed to women: "In women too we must postulate a somatic sexual excitation and a state in which this excitation becomes a psychical stimulus—

libido—and provokes the urge to the specific action to which voluptuous feeling is attached" (109). Anxiety neurosis occurs, in both men and women, when somatic excitation cannot be worked over psychically. Neurasthenia occurs whenever adequate discharge of excitation ("normal coition, carried out in the most favorable conditions," 109) is replaced by a less somatically adequate one (e.g., masturbation). In the case of masturbation, the nerve endings are not properly unloaded, and the somatic tension will continue unabated, producing the symptoms of neurasthenia.

Beard located the source of neurasthenic sensitivity and irritability in the cultural conditions pressing on the minds and bodies of individuals. In Freud, a different kind of neurasthenic mechanism is being hypothesized. It is the flesh itself that carries the etiological burden of neurasthenia. While the toxic influences of physical illness, depressive affects, and overwork may contribute to a general fatigue, it is only when the nervous system is unable to discharge accumulated somatic tension through a sexually adequate action that the symptoms of neurasthenia are produced. It is not a crude biology that Freud nominates here; more provocatively, it is a sexualized nervous system that cultivates neurasthenic symptomology. It is the nerve endings in the seminal vesicles that play a pivotal role in the adequate circulation and discharge of somatic and psychic excitation, and therefore in the management of a certain degree of bodily and mental well-being.

Rather than sounding a critical warning against a theory that endeavors to place a penis-brain reflex arc at the explanatory center of a psychological model, I would like to look a little more closely at what is entailed ontologically in this hypothesis. That is, I wish to put to one side the alarm, mockery, or incredulity that the juxtaposition nerves-penis-cortex-psyche would normally elicit in certain critical and political circles, and listen for what kinds of useful critical and political tenets such a juxtaposition may be laying before us. Is Freud's circuit of nerves-penis-cortex-psyche an assemblage of self-contained elements arranged in determinable relations of cause and effect? Or is it a psychosomatic economy within which the identity of each element (nerve, penis, cortex, psyche) is constituted as an effect of that economic structuration? If it is the latter (which I argue it is), then the identity of penis and cortex cannot be known in advance of, or outside of, their excited, circuitous relations. Moreover, the difference between biology (penis and cortex) on the one hand and the psyche on the other cannot be determined such that we can know with absolute certainty that the juxtaposition of seminal vesicles and psyche means that the first term prescribes and subdues the second term. If the psyche is already of the circuitry that encompasses cortex, nerves, and penis, then we have a system of mutual constitution from which no particular element emerges as the originary, predetermining term. In such a network the psyche is indeed cortical, nervous, seminal, but so too are the seminal vesicles constituted at their core as psychic, so too is the cortex irreducibly sexualized. Charges of neurological determinism inadequately grasp the ontological and relational complexity that this Freudian model entails.

A theoretical caveat concerning relationality is necessary here. The structure I am elucidating in Freud could be called a relational or distributed network only when certain ontological conditions have been met. It seems to me that the logic of distribution is critically valuable only as it approximates a Derridean notion of dissemination or *différance*—that is, a distribution or relationality that it constitutive of its component elements (E. A. Wilson 1998). The distribution of already intact entities (penis, cortex, psyche) into part or subentities is not what is entailed in my reading of Freud. In this second, problematic sense of distribution, the difficulty of a singular, localized presence (penis, cortex, psyche) is not addressed by distributing that presence secondarily into fragments, networks, or mobile assemblages. Distribution has to be originary and constitutive. Freud was cognizant of the need to think about neurological distribution carefully. He made his concerns explicit in his little-read but highly regarded monograph on aphasia (Freud 1891), where he argues strongly against Wernicke's theory that aphasia is a disruption to speech centers. Freud maintains that such a theory doesn't sufficiently revise the localizationist tendencies of phrenology: "Considering the tendency of earlier medical periods to localize whole mental faculties . . . in certain areas of the brain, it was bound to appear as a great advance when Wernicke declared that only the simplest psychic elements, i.e., the various sensory perceptions, could be localized in the cortex . . . But does one not in principle make the same mistake, irrespective of whether one tries to localize a complicated concept, a whole mental faculty or a psychic element?" (54–55). Freud's subsequent, unpublished musings on neurasthenia try out this hypothesis about neurological circuits, association, and influence in less orthodox territory.

In a draft paper in the Fliess correspondence, Freud (1895a) extends his model of neurasthenia beyond the actual neuroses to take account of the psychoneurosis melancholia. He makes a case for "neurasthenic melancholia," where excessive masturbation has chronically reduced somatic excitation. This weakening of the somatic system results in a libidinal impoverishment that is experienced psychically as melancholia. The strange etiology and itinerary of the symptoms of neurasthenic melancholia are documented in a diagram that maps the circulation of excitation from the soma to the psyche and back. The end-organ, spinal center, ego, and sexual object are linked via the movement of sexual tension and "voluptuous feelings" across the somatic-psychical boundary. This diagram in figure 1 is a map of the psychosomatic structure that is disrupted in cases of neur-

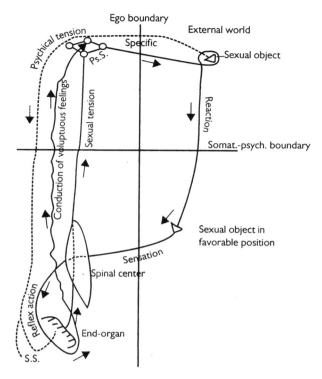

Figure 1. Schematic picture of sexuality. Reprinted with the permission of the Institute of Psychoanalysis from Freud 1895a, 202.

asthenia. Low somatic tension in the end-organ (caused by immoderate masturbation) leads to a melancholic inhibition of the psyche, instinctual impoverishment, and pain.

Freud's treatment of neurology in this model is interesting in two regards. First, he gives prominent place to the neurologically lowly: the peripheral nervous system and the reflex arc (more of which in chapter 4). In this model, not everything is cortical, cognitive, knowing. Second, the nervous system is thoroughly corporeal. Freud's neurons are functioning more like flesh and blood than like cerebral units: "There may come about *an in-drawing* (as it were) *in the psychical sphere*, which produces an effect of suction upon the adjoining amounts of excitation. The associated neurones are obliged to give up their excitation, *which produces pain*. Uncoupling associations is always painful. There sets in an impoverishment in excitation . . . an *internal haemorrhage*, as it were—which shows itself in the other instincts and functions. This in-drawing operates inhibitingly, like a *wound*, in a manner analogous to pain" (1895a, 205–206).

Weakness of the soma (produced by masturbation, in the case of men, or cultural constraint on sexuality, in the case of women) instigates a melancholic weakening of the psyche not because the somatic governs the psychic, but because the soma and psyche are ontologically integrated. Weakness in one part of this psychosomatic system will be disseminated generally. We have already seen the corollary of this in the introduction: conversion hysteria is somatic weakening instigated by psychic trauma. The *Studies on Hysteria*, where Freud first investigates conversion hysteria, were written at about the same time as this work on neurasthenia. In all this early writing Freud is mapping out (sometimes convincingly, sometimes not) a neurologically grounded psychosomatic structure in which the relation between elements rather than the elements themselves determines the character of that structure. What we come to know as psyche, cortex, melancholia, penis, or reflex is an effect of networked influence. Neurons are libidinized; nervous systems trade pathologies; neuroses sometimes short-circuit systems of representation; sexuality circulates not just within the end-organ, but also through the ego and the external world; cultural habits become obligated to biology, and biology becomes obligated to the psyche. The introduction and this opening chapter have been using these early Freudian maps to argue that neurological material is more confident, flexible, resilient, and assertive than many critics have yet acknowledged.[5] This model of a vigorous (rather than dictatorial) neurology is expanded in the following chapters in relation to sexuality, affect, and evolution.

The important critical task in relation to Freud's theories of neurasthenia is not to accuse Freud of falling back to the biological to explain psychological or cultural symptomology, but rather to investigate what kind of ontological structure Freud is entertaining when he suggests that neurons are "obliged" by the psyche to give up their excitation. What is the character of this psychosomatic structure such that soma and psyche are bound by obligation rather than unilateral control? While the term *obligation* is usually enlisted to designate a binding relation between people, or more broadly, between two agents, Freud's use of the term here implies no such human or conscious action. This is not a metaphorical use of obligation, if metaphorical is taken in the narrow sense of bringing the meaning of obligation to bear on psychosomatic action when it is properly applicable to another domain (social relations). Freud's use of obligation at the level of neuropsychic interchange denatures the human- and conscious-centric sense with which obligation is used elsewhere. The effect is not to render neurological action knowable via obligation, but to make obligation curious via its association with the microbiological.[6] Neurological obligation, then, is one way of understanding a relation between psyche and soma in which there is a mutuality of influence, a mutuality that is interminable and constitutive. Under

Freud, it makes little sense to say that neurons predetermine the psychological realm when the neurons themselves are already bound to the psyche in a relation of duty. Likewise, the psyche cannot be in command of neurology if psychological effects depend on the movement of neural excitation.

Freud is postulating a melancholic ontology of pain, hemorrhaging, and wounding within which psychical forces and somatic forces are mutually and constitutively bound. The system that he hints at here is a circuitry founded on the logic of breaching (Derrida 1978). That is, the identity of the circuit's components (neuron, psyche, melancholia), and the character of the circuit itself, are forged through a forceful, painful interrelation. In such a structure the critical problematic of determinism has been displaced: it becomes meaningless to charge that psychic forces are governed by the soma if the soma itself is already psychic, cognitive, and affective. The vectors of governance (what determines what?) are here fully disseminated—which is not to say that they are undecidable (an unsystematic array of random associations), but rather that they are not delimitable within conventional parameters of cause and effect, origin and derivation. The action of neurology (source) on psychology (outcome) has been routed, by Freud, through the accountability of the source to the outcome. In such a structure, critical anxieties about (and orthodox ambitions for) incontestable determinism have nowhere to land.

For Freud, neurasthenic symptoms are somatic in nature; perhaps more precisely, we could identify them as nervous. They speak to an irritability and oversensitivity that is irreducibly psychobiological. Kramer saw as much in Lucy. Through Freud, I want to highlight how purely cultural explanations of neurasthenia (or depression) may generate the very biological austerity they wish to contest. Too easy an attribution of neurasthenia or depression to cultural constraints will have a reductive effect on nervousness; it will contain neurology to the role of a substrate or foundation to which an already anxious psyche attaches itself or onto which an exhausting cultural milieu writes itself. It will set up a structure within which neurology is affectless matter and nervousness and melancholia are immaterial psychical states radically adrift from not only the nervous system but also the digestive, circulatory, and excretory systems. Both anxiety and pain—two dominant concerns in Freud's writing in the 1890s—expose (often all too acutely) the kinship among the psychic, nervous, digestive, circulatory, and excretory systems. This circuitry is explored further in the next chapter.

Through a precarious biological elucidation of neurasthenia, Freud manages a displacement of biological determinism that is more thoroughgoing than most nonbiological hypotheses can deliver. I would attribute the efficacy of Freud's model not to the importation of cultural, metaphorical, or discursive action, but to his close and steadily fixed focus on the malleable actuality of neurological matter. The critical potency of such a biological reiteration is something I wish to pursue further in Kramer's account of neurology and depression.

Stress and Neurological Kindling

We are in the midst of a neurasthenic epidemic similar to that documented by Beard: the epidemic of stress. In ways that are similar to Beard's hypotheses concerning neurasthenia, stress is commonly attributed to the over-stimulation, overwork, worry, and deprivations of a late capitalist, technologically oriented, information-hungry culture (Griggers 1997). And like neurasthenic symptoms, the symptoms of stress are not simply widespread, they are a naturalized aspect of our everyday lives (Goodall 1996; Martin 1997; Showalter 1997).

In one of the middle chapters of *Listening to Prozac*, Kramer (1993) asks us to consider a series of hypotheses about the nature of depression that call on the ubiquitous nature of stress. Robert Post, Kramer tells us, is a biologist who is trained in the chemistry of the neuron, but who also has an interest in the behavior of clinically depressed patients. Post is particularly interested in manic-depressive (bipolar) patients who have become "rapid cyclers." These are patients in whom "mood seems to have lost its attachment to any psychological stimulus whatsoever" and "affect has become utterly dissociated from their experience of the everyday world" (108). Post found that over the course of some years, the time between depressive episodes for each patient had decreased and each depressive episode was being provoked by an increasingly minor psychological event. Eventually, the depression had taken on an independent course: it was initiated and maintained independently of events in the environment—it had become "functionally autonomous."

Post was attracted to a long-standing model of epilepsy as a way of explaining this kind of functional autonomy in rapid cyclers. It has been demonstrated experimentally that epileptic seizures can be induced in normal animals through exposure to a series of small, initially nontraumatic electrical currents. The first shock does not induce a seizure, but over time, without increasing the level of the shock, the animal begins to respond with seizures that are initially small and contained but that eventually become more severe and widespread. Once the brain has been so "kindled," smaller and smaller electrical shocks will induce seizure. Moreover, this kindling is documented in the brain. The application of electrical current changes the synaptic connections in the brain, and these changes in neural anatomy are evident before manifest seizures begin.

Following Post, Kramer presents a kindling model for the etiology and course of depression:

> Manic depression, and perhaps all depression . . . is a progressive, probably lifelong disorder. It can be induced in normals. The induction can take place through a series of small stimuli, none of which at first causes overt symptoms. The latency to fully expressed illness can be long, and the absence of overt symptoms is no guarantee that the underlying process is not underway. Illness, once expressed, can become responsive to ever smaller stimuli and, in time, independent of stimuli altogether. The expression of the disorder becomes more complex over time. Even the early stimuli are translated into anatomical, difficult-to-reverse changes in the brain. Different treatments are appropriate to different stages of the illness. Early and prolonged intervention is crucial. (1993, 114)

Maybe the brains of traumatized people have been stressed in such a way that it leaves them vulnerable, not to seizures, but to attacks of depression. A substantial trauma early in life (in Lucy's case, the shocking death of her mother) may be sufficient to weaken the neurological system so that this person becomes susceptible to depression at a later date following a relatively minor trauma.[7] Or, more worryingly, perhaps the brain may be kindled for depression through the stresses of everyday life. In her autobiographical best-seller *Prozac Nation*, Elizabeth Wurtzel (1995) offers this kindling model as an explanation for her own depression: "It's not just that an a priori imbalance can make you depressed. It's that years and years of exogenous depression (a malaise caused by external events) can actually fuck up your internal chemistry so much that you need a drug to get it working properly again. Had I been treated by a competent therapist at the onset of my depression, perhaps its mere kindling would not have turned into a nightmarish psychic bonfire, and I might not have arrived at the point, a decade later, where I needed medication just to be able to get out of bed in the morning" (346).

Like the neurasthenic patient, the depressive patient is a casualty to nervous weakening. And just like Freud's model of neurasthenia, Kramer's kindling model of depression locates psychopathology directly (or "actually") in somatic encoding: "What distinguishes this view of depression from, say, traditional psychoanalytic models is the recognition that scars are not, or not only, in cognitive memory. It is not merely a question of inner conflict . . . The scar consists of changed anatomy and chemistry in the brain. Some of that brain change is memory: presumably recollected thought and emotion are encoded in ways that bear resemblance to the kindling model . . . In this sense, social inhibition and rejection-sensitivity are both memory.

That is, they do not *stem from* a (cognitive, emotion-laden, conflicted) memory of trauma; they represent or just *are* memories of trauma" (1993, 123–124).

Kramer suggests that there is a direct neurocognitive scarring in some depressed patients that circumvents the usual pathways of signification and symptom formation. These depressive symptoms (like neurasthenic symptoms) are not amenable to the interpretive strategies of psychotherapeutic technique: they don't symbolize anything, nor do they originate in unconscious or infantile events.[8] For Kramer, the utility of Prozac as a therapeutic intervention in such cases of depression is indisputable.

Neurological Determinations

A somatically grounded account of depression (such as Kramer's kindling model) would normally promote a theory in which the soma determines the psyche. For example, Kramer explains how the behavioral effects of Prozac reoriented his own views on the nature of depression: "I called this phenomenon 'listening to Prozac.' As I thought about it, I began to understand how far my own listening to Prozac extended. Spending time with patients who responded to Prozac had transformed my views about what makes people the way they are. I had come to see inborn, biologically determined temperament where before I had seen slowly acquired, history-laden character" (1993, xv).

This passage is frequently cited by reviewers and commentators as evidence of Kramer's biologically determinist agenda. I would argue, however, that what is being documented in this early, introductory comment is Kramer's reevaluation of his own intuitive attachment to purely psychological models of depression and subjectivity.[9] *Listening to Prozac* does not simplistically replace psychological or cultural determinism with biological determinism; more carefully, it opens up the very nature of determination (i.e., certainty, termination, resolution) to interrogation.[10] As Kramer's clinical cases and empirical examples disclose, the logic of biochemical determination (like the logic of mood itself) is multivalent: some people feel "better than well" when taking Prozac; some people find that a previously cherished or familiar part of their personality is attenuated by Prozac, and some experience this change as a loss while others find themselves happily reoriented to a new aspect of themselves; some people become seriously agitated by certain doses of Prozac, others barely respond to it yet are immeasurably helped by another ssri antidepressant. And all of these responses may vary over time in any given individual. Even Prozac's most notorious side effects—diminished libido and delayed orgasm—manifest in ways that are distressing, hardly noticeable, somewhat tolerable, intractable, readily mastered; or perhaps these side effects do not appear at all.[11] Nowhere in *Listening to Prozac* is neurology—with or without pharmaceutical assistance—deployed as a univocal determinant of human psychology. In fact, Kramer's attentive suturing of clinical, experimental, and chemical accounts of neurology has the effect of putting all manner of biological and cultural certainties back into analytic circulation: "My aim was not to settle a moral debate but to make such a debate seem unavoidable, unsettling, and difficult to resolve" (1997a, 318).

Importantly for the argument I am endeavoring to build here, the unavoidable, unsettling, difficult to resolve character of neurology is articulated by Kramer through close, empirical attention to neurology itself. As it was by Freud. For both these authors, their critical sensibilities are animated and amplified by neurological detail. It is the careful determination of neurological effects (What kind of influence? When? Under what conditions? With what constraints? By which pathway?) that displaces classical neurological determinism. This is the case even when, as with Freud, much of the neurological detail is empirically antiquated. What makes the juxtaposition of Kramer and Freud critically instructive is that both demonstrate how neurological determinism is most powerfully contested through neurological intimacy.

Critical and political responses to *Listening to Prozac* have been much less animated by, indeed much less interested in, neurological detail.[12] Camilla Griggers's (1997) critique of psychopharmacology and psychiatry (and Kramer's *Listening to Prozac* in particular) is exemplary of such responses. Her Deleuzian antipsychiatry forgoes a close examination of neuropsychological events; notably, she extends the nervous system beyond neurological matters to encompass Michael Taussig's formulation of a generalized "Nervous System." Following Taussig, Griggers designates the nervous system as "a system that screens itself with the illusion of a nerve center and hierarchy of control within the individual self, a system that makes hermeneutics its property while projecting it as the property of the individual subject. The nervous system is the historical outcome of a legacy of disorganized violences veiled as organized progress by modernity's ideology of an ordered machinic socius. As such, it now energizes a postmodern regime of arbitrariness and planning in the post–World War II reconfiguration of state, market, and transnational corporations" (107).

In Griggers's ensuing analysis, the phrase nervous system refers indeterminately to a biological system and to a history of circulating violences. This indeterminacy serves the purpose of breaking through the conventional sequestration of biological systems from historical, social, and economic systems. With this rhetorical move the nervous system is opened up to its historical, social, and economic determinations. Nonetheless, the breaching effects of this indeterminacy are channeled by Griggers in only certain directions: from the historical, social, and economic onto the biological. Although the debts that neurology owes to history, culture, and economics are expansively articulated, the correlative obligations of history, culture, and economics to neurology are overlooked. Because it remains axiomatic for Griggers that neurological and pharmaceutical determinations are delimited and delimiting, the facilitating effects of neurology and chemistry on history, culture, and economy are obstructed—or perhaps more accurately, these effects are rendered inarticulate. Unwilling to sustain a focus on neurological detail (as it "reterritorializes breakdown as individuality"), Griggers's analysis loses sight of the particularities, modulations, and natural vicissitudes of the nervous system. And so, despite the carefully managed terminological ambiguity, the nervous system as a biological system is removed from the circuit of ontological dissemination. Historical, social, and economic determinations are thus protected from a more profound determinacy, and the notion of neurology as arid materiality is entrenched further.

To return to Kramer's problematic concerning serotonergic pathways and a mother's death: Griggers demonstrates how cortical pathways may be breached by nonneurological forces (serotonergic pathways may be disrupted by the psychocultural trauma of a mother's death), but the disseminating influence of neurology is foreclosed (Can historical, cultural, or economic events be serotonergic?). For Griggers, the influence of psychopharmaceuticals is primarily suppressive; a serotonergic history will always be a history of normalization. Indeed, she urges the female subject to take unilateral control over her serotonergic determinations: "Whether or not she uses psychotropic chemical treatments to [deterritorialize desire and subjectification] is not the issue. The issue is whether the psychopharmacological machine is channeling her or whether she is in some way channeling it toward a historically informed collective notion of what would constitute a meaningful social response to being subject to, and becoming-woman within, postmodern culture's agitated nervous system" (1997, 133).

It is precisely this figuration of channeling and control that I am trying to displace; via Freud and Kramer, I have been trying to think of neurological and serotonergic determinations as less catastrophically doctrinaire. For it is not clear to me that the best way to support the (important) argument that "pharmaceutical treatment alone can never and should never stand in the place of a conscious understanding of the social history of violence, and of one's own relation to that history" (Griggers 1997, 144) is to keep serotonergic pathways under the thumb of historical and social determination. I have suggested that the rubric of obligation may be a more instructive way to structure the relation between serotonergic pathways and the death of one's mother.

As Kramer attempts to write with (rather than against) neurological determinism, what emerges in *Listening to Prozac* is the full efficacy of neurological writing. By placing psychical effects in an intimate alliance with the anatomical configurations of the nervous system, Kramer's kindling model elucidates one particular mode of neurology's articulate nature. Not only is depression neurological, but neurology is also depressive. Rather than simply leading to depression, neurological matter itself may become weakened, neurasthenic, depressive: neurology doesn't stand to one side of the effects it facilitates. This kind of neurology sometimes breaks down; this kind of neurology needs words and chemicals and affective attunement to keep working; this weakened and depressed neurology underscores the literate and sometimes melancholic nature of biology in general.

Political engagements with this kind of neurology will be different from those we have become used to in feminist, antipsychiatric, and social constructionist literatures. This neurology—articulate, obligated, libidinized—may be a resource for theoretical endeavor, rather than the dangerous and inert substrate against which criticism launches itself. One of the central difficulties in using neurology critically has been the tendency to equate the nervous system with the central nervous system and to equate the central nervous system with cognition—desexualized, calculating, and autocratic. In the chapters that follow I move between the central and peripheral nervous systems and among the cognitive, the affective, and the unknowing, in an attempt to build a critically empathic alliance with neurology.

· · · · · · · ·   2

· · · · · · · ·   The Brain in the Gut

· · · · · · · ·   When Freud first meets Frau Emmy von N., she is
depressed, insomniac, hallucinating, and suffering from chronic pain. Frau
Emmy has endured numerous hysterical afflictions over a fourteen-year
period, and she has undertaken a variety of treatments unsuccessfully. By
good fortune, she can be hypnotized easily, so she becomes the first patient
whom Freud treats with Breuer's new therapeutic method: massage, hypnosis, abreaction.

Freud sends Frau Emmy to a nursing home, where he visits her twice a
day (morning and evening). At each visit he massages her whole body and
hypnotizes her. In the beginning he uses hypnotic states simply to get her to
sleep and to offer general suggestions that will remove her hysterical symptomology: "She is an excellent subject for hypnotism. I had only to hold up a
finger in front of her and order her to go to sleep, and she sank back with a
dazed and confused look. I suggested that she should sleep well, that all her
symptoms should get better, and so on" (Breuer and Freud 1895, 50–51).

A few days into the treatment Freud refines his technique; he asks Frau
Emmy to talk while she is under hypnosis. He begins by inquiring into her
emotional state: Why is it that she is so readily frightened? Frau Emmy
responds with a series of traumatic episodes from her childhood: how her
siblings used to throw dead animals at her; how she unexpectedly saw her
sister in her coffin; how her brother terrified her by dressing up in a sheet like
a ghost; and how she saw her aunt in her coffin and her aunt's jaw suddenly
dropped. Over a period of eight weeks Freud investigates these and other
episodes of fright, removing with a hypnotic suggestion the "impression" left
by each episode. He learns that he is unable to remove the frightful impres-

sions en masse with a general suggestion; instead, he must listen to each episode in its entirety and then remove its hysterical imprint individually.

One of Frau Emmy's persistent symptoms is gastric pain. Early in the treatment Freud asks her, when hypnotized, about the origin of her gastric discomfort: "Her answer, which she gave rather grudgingly, was that she did not know. I requested her to remember by tomorrow. She then said in a definitely grumbling tone that I was not to keep on asking her where this and that came from, but to let her tell me what she had to say. I fell in with this, and she went on without preface: 'When they carried him [my husband] out, I could not believe he was dead' " (63).

The next morning, Freud finds that Frau Emmy has slept badly and her gastric pain has returned. Under hypnosis she confirms that for a long time after her husband's death she had lost her appetite and had forced herself to eat out of a sense of duty. Recognizing that the gastric pains had begun at this time, Freud acts to remove the imprint of her husband's sudden death, the grief, and the forced ingestion: "I then removed her gastric pains by stroking her a few times across the epigastrium [the region of the abdomen above the stomach]" (64).

Toward the end of the treatment there is another episode of indigestion. One day Freud surprises Frau Emmy in the act of throwing her lunch into the garden. He soon discovers that she has been eating very little, and though she doesn't seem underweight he nevertheless deems it worthwhile "to aim at feeding her up a little" (81). Frau Emmy complains that, like her father, she eats very little, and that she is unable to drink water or minerals as it ruins her digestion for days on end. Instead, she drinks only thick fluids like milk, coffee, or cocoa. Freud considers that this demonstrates "all the signs of a neurotic choice"; he takes a urine sample and finds that "it was highly concentrated and overcharged with urates" (81). He instructs her to drink more and he increases the amount of food she is given. This directive produces uncharacteristic insolence in Frau Emmy: " 'I'll do it because you ask me to,' she said, 'but I can tell you in advance that it will turn out badly, because it is contrary to my nature' " (81). The next day, Freud returns to find that Frau Emmy has followed his instructions, but that this has indeed had a toxic effect on her: "I found Frau Emmy . . . lying in a profoundly depressed state and in a very ungracious mood. She complained of having very violent gastric pains" (81).

At the time of Frau Emmy's treatment (1888), Freud is "completely under the sway of Bernheim's book on suggestion" (Breuer and Freud 1895, 77). His methods bear little resemblance to the psychoanalytic technique that he will develop in the years ahead. In particular, he does not investigate the symbolism of the episodes he is hypnotically modifying,[1] and he relies on didactic interventions to a much greater extent than he will later on. So on finding Frau Emmy depressed and in pain, Freud simply attempts to assure her that it is impossible to ruin one's digestion by drinking water or eating more and that her gastric pain is due to anxiety. At this moment, Freud finds himself at the limit of his technique:

> It was clear that this explanation of mine made not the slightest impression on her. For when, soon afterwards, I tried to put her to sleep, for the first time I failed to bring about hypnosis; and the furious look she cast at me convinced me that she was in open rebellion and that the situation was very grave. I gave up trying to hypnotize her, and announced that I would give her twenty-four hours to think things over and accept the view that her gastric pains came only from her fear. At the end of this time I would ask her whether she was still of the opinion that her digestion could be ruined for a week by drinking a glass of mineral water and eating a modest meal; if she said yes, I would ask her to leave. (81–82)

The next day, Freud finds her "docile and submissive" (82). When asked about the origin of her gastric pains, she replies, "I think they come from my anxiety, but only because you say so" (82). Under hypnosis she recalls a number of disgusting episodes concerning food and drink (being made to eat a cold meal by her mother; eating with a brother who had a habit of expectorating across plates into a spittoon; contracting a gastric catarrh from bad drinking water when young). By now Freud seems to have regained his therapeutic equilibrium: "I naturally made a thorough clearance of this whole array of agencies of disgust . . . the therapeutic effect of these discoveries under hypnosis was immediate and lasting. She did *not* starve herself for a week but the very next day she ate and drank without any difficulty" (82–83).

I use the case of Frau Emmy as a starting point for thinking about nervousness in the gut because it focuses on how a husband's death, a patient's resistances and fears, and an analyst's authority can be gastrically internal—not just ideational or cerebral. In this chapter I explore the nervous condition of the gut. What are the specifics of the enteric nervous system that innervates the digestive tract? How does this system regulate, and how is it regulated by, psychological events? Psychoanalysis has had plenty to say about the psychology of the openings of the digestive tract (orality, anality) but much less about the processes in between. Despite the large amount of clinical and anecdotal evidence that points to the gut's highly mobile, highly sensitive psychological nature, the psychodynamics of this part of the nervous body remain understudied. Frau Emmy's case provides an initial schema for thinking about the nervous system beyond the head; it turns our attention to how the nervous system innervates the entire body, and how distal parts of the body (such as the stomach) have the capacity for psychological action.

It seems that contemporary biomedical research on the nervous system in the gut is being mobilized to disaggregate any such affiliation between psyche and the somatic periphery. The influence of psychological events on gastrointestinal disorders appears to be widely recognized, yet this influence is usually kept at a distance from the gut—sequestered in the brain or in the vaguest possible terms attributed to external, social factors such as stress. In this chapter I map out this antipsychological tendency, and then explore aspects of one possible affiliation of psyche and neurogastroenterology (specifically, depressive events and gastrointestinal disorder); I focus on Freud's psychological techniques before they have been dissociated from explanation through the nerves and the soma,[2] on neurogastroenterology as it attempts to detach itself from psychological influence, and on clinical data as these demonstrate the imaginary anatomy of the gut. That is, I am interested in accounts of the gut that struggle with ambivalence and incoherence about psyche-soma relations. I am interested in accounts of the gut before the threads of psychic, neurological, and microbiological affiliation have been severed in the service of more reasonable, more credibly scientific, or more properly psychoanalytic demands. Following on from the analysis of neuropsychic circuits in chapter 1, I hope to build a schema of the gut that is legible in both transferential and enterological terms.

The Enteric Nervous System

The enteric nervous system (ENS) is a complex network of nerves that encases and innervates the digestive tract from the esophagus to the anus. The ENS is anatomically extensive: the small intestine in humans has as many neurons as the spinal cord; "add on the nerve cells of the esophagus, stomach, and large intestine and you find that we have more nerve cells in our bowel than in our spine. We have more nerve cells in our gut than in the entire remainder of our peripheral nervous system" (Gershon 1998, xiii). The ENS is anatomically and biochemically more similar to the central nervous system (CNS) than it is to any other part of the peripheral nervous system to which it belongs. Unlike other parts of the peripheral nervous system, the ENS may act independently of CNS innervation. For these reasons, the ENS has been variously named "the brain of the gut," "the enteric minibrain," and "the second brain."[3]

There has been dispute over the taxonomic status of the ENS. For some time, the ENS was seen as part of the parasympathetic branch of the autonomic nervous system (ANS).[4] That is, the ENS was thought to be a fairly simple relay system for digestive processes. Recent research suggests a more complex picture; Goyal and Hirano (1996), for example, argue that the ENS "may perhaps best be regarded as a displaced part of the central nervous system that retains communication with it through sympathetic and parasympathetic afferent and efferent neurons" (1106). There is general agreement among those working in the field that the ENS is an ANS system distinct from the sympathetic and parasympathetic branches, and that the ENS "exhibits a complexity that is found in no other group of neurons outside the central nervous system" (Furness and Costa 1987, 1).[5]

There are a number of biochemical, anatomical, and functional findings about the ENS that have established the character of this part of the human nervous system:

1. There are two major nerve networks (plexuses) in the ENS. The myenteric plexus controls the motility of the muscles in the gut wall; the submucous plexus, which is most developed in the small intestine, regulates blood flow and glandular secretion into the lumen (internal cavity) of the small intestine. Both plexuses vary anatomically among species;[6] they vary along the length of the gut of any one species (e.g., the myenteric plexus is especially dense in the rectal portion of the intestine in humans); and they vary according to the age of the organism. Within each plexus there are three major classes of neurons: sensory neurons (which detect changes in thermal, chemical, and mechanical conditions in the gut), motor neurons (which control vasodilation and muscle movement), and interneurons (which make associative and integrative links between other enteric neurons). The ENS also contains a large number of glial-like cells (nonconducting nerve cells that protect and support other neurons). All these ENS neurons are functionally and morphologically similar to the neurons in the brain. Gershon (1999) suggests that the anatomical and chemical similarities between the ENS and the CNS mean that the ENS is vulnerable to the same pathologies as the CNS. Alzheimer's and Parkinson's disease, for example, affect the ENS in much the same way they affect the brain: "Both the Lewy bodies associated with Parkinson's disease and the amyloid plaques and neurofibrillary tangles identified with Alzheimer's disease have been found in the bowels of patients with these conditions. It is conceivable that Alzheimer's disease, so difficult to diagnose in the absence of autopsy data, may some day be routinely identified by rectal biopsy" (35). The ENS, then, is an anatomically heterogeneous and functionally specialized nervous system that bears a stronger resemblance to the CNS than to other peripheral systems: "Unlike other autonomic ganglia [bundles of nerves] that function mainly as relay dis-

tribution centers for signals transmitted from the CNS, ENS ganglia are inter-connected to form a nervous system with mechanisms for integration and processing of information like those found in the brain" (Woods, Alpers, and Andrews 1999, II7).

2. The ENS contains every class of neurotransmitter that is found in the CNS. Serotonin has been found to be a particularly important neurotransmitter in the ENS. The vast majority of the body's serotonin—Kim and Camilleri (2000) suggest about 95 percent—is made, stored, and metabolized in the gut, and most of the serotonin in the blood is derived from the gut. Serotonin is thought to be important in a whole range of digestive processes, especially intestinal secretion, peristaltic activity (it stimulates both contraction and relaxation of the intestinal muscles), nausea, and vomiting.[7] Gastrointestinal disruption (e.g., constipation or nausea) is a common side effect of SSRI medication; correspondingly, pharmaceuticals that regulate serotonin in the gut have been found to be useful in the management of functional gastrointestinal disorders such as irritable bowel syndrome. By 1999 at least thirty neurotransmitters had been identified in the brain and all of these are also found in the ENS. These include amines (acetylecholine, norepinephrine, serotonin), amino acids, purines, peptides, and nitric oxide.

3. There is relatively little in the way of direct nervous traffic between the gut and the brain. The vagus nerves, which connect the brain and the bowel, have only a few thousand fibers. Moreover, most of the vagal fibers are afferent; that is, they relay information from the gut to the brain. There is very little direct innervation in the other direction, from the brain to the gut. There are over a hundred million nerve cells in the human small intestine. Most enteric neurons, therefore, are connected to other enteric neurons, rather than to the brain or the spinal cord. The ENS is somewhat sequestered—anatomically and biochemically—from CNS influence. Gershon (1999) tends to overstate this independence: "The enteric nervous system does not necessarily follow commands it receives from the brain or the spinal cord; nor does it inevitably send the information it receives back to them. The enteric nervous system can, when it chooses, process data its sensory receptors pick up all by themselves, and it can act on the basis of those data to activate a set of effectors [muscles, glands, blood vessels] that it alone controls. The enteric nervous system is thus not a slave of the brain but a contrarian, independent spirit in the nervous organization of the body. It is a rebel, the only element of the peripheral nervous system that can elect not to do the bidding of the brain or spinal cord" (17).

This notion of a maverick ENS creates the impression of a much greater separation of the ENS from the CNS than actually exists.[8] The relation between the ENS and the CNS—largely independent yet indirectly connected (displaced, as

Goyal and Hirano suggest)—is a difficult one to conceptualize. Woods et al. (1999) figure this relation in computational and cybernetic terms:

> The earlier concept [of ENS innervation] placed the "computer" entirely within the brain, whereas, current concepts place "microprocessor" circuits within the wall of the gut in close proximity to the effector systems [muscles, glands, blood vessels] . . . Rather than having the neural control circuits packed exclusively within the CNS and transmitting every byte of control information over long transmission lines, vertebrate animals have most of the circuits for autonomic feedback control located in close proximity to the effector systems . . . In this respect, the ENS is analogous to a microcomputer with its own independent software, whereas the brain is like a larger mainframe with extended memory and processing circuits that receive information from and issue commands to the enteric computer. (117–118)

The difficulties of the extended computer analogy (nerve cells do not, for example, transmit information in a manner similar to either wires or silicon chips) tend to obscure Woods et al.'s attempt to refigure the relation of enteric and central nervous systems (where local circuits feed into larger arrays, but without being governed by them). There is some recognition in the field that conventional schemata of brain control of peripheral events (i.e., top-down administration by the cortex) do not hold in relation to the ENS. There is a tendency, therefore, to figure the ENS as independent of CNS control. It remains an ongoing difficulty in the field to know how the disarticulation of the ENS from the CNS can be conceptualized more satisfactorily: if conventional hierarchies no longer hold in the same kinds of ways, and if notions of independence and autonomy tend to replicate the same problematic ground, how can the interrelation of these nervous systems be conceptualized?

4. Different parts of the digestive tract are innervated by different parts of the nervous system. The CNS regulates the upper portions (esophagus and stomach) and the distal portions (anorectum) of the digestive tract; there is much less direct CNS innervation of the small intestine and colon, which are primarily under ENS control. It is CNS-regulated digestive processes that are most often available to consciousness (swallowing, the beginnings of gastric digestion, defecation) and that have been most available to psychological (especially psychoanalytic) speculation. The portions of the gut regulated mainly by the ENS (stomach, small intestine, upper colon) tend to remain outside awareness until they break down (diarrhea, constipation, irritable bowel syndrome). Nonetheless, the activities of the middle portions of the gut have been frequently reported in psychological contexts. Many nineteenth-century cases of hysteria, anxiety neurosis, neurasthenia, and

melancholia are concerned with disruptions to digestion. Early on, for example, Freud reports to Fliess a typical neurosis case, of Herr von F., who is losing his "liveliness and zest"; his condition is "characterized by bad digestion—that is, by disinclination for food and by belching [*Aufstoßen*] and sluggish stools" (Freud 1894a, 194).[9] This patient's neurotic state is intermittent, but he is able to gauge impending nervous weakness by the return of belching. Much later, in one of his most accomplished case histories (Wolf Man), Freud notes that "disturbance of appetite should be regarded as the very first of the patient's neurotic illnesses" (1918, 98). In contemporary clinical contexts, disruptions of the stomach, small intestine, and colon are central to diagnoses of somatoform disorders.[10] Somatization disorder (the contemporary psychiatric term for hysteria), for example, requires that in addition to pain in at least four different bodily sites or related to four different bodily functions, "there also must be a history of at least two gastrointestinal symptoms other than pain . . . Most individuals with the disorder describe the presence of nausea and abdominal bloating. Vomiting, diarrhea, and food intolerance are less common. Gastrointestinal complaints often lead to frequent X-ray examinations and can result in abdominal surgery that in retrospect was unnecessary" (American Psychiatric Association 1994, 446). The ENS, then, is no less allied with psychological states than the CNS, and the gut is innervated by a number of events: neuroenteric, endocrinological, cerebral, affective, dysthymic, and transferential.

Psychoenterology

The importance of psychological events to the functioning of the gut is widely recognized: "Irritable bowel syndrome is associated in some patients with altered GI [gastrointestinal] transit, a variety of manometric abnormalities in the small and large intestine, increased visceral sensation, and psychological features including depression and anxiety" (Kim and Camilleri 2000, 2702). Indeed, Talley's (2001) guidelines in *The Lancet* for the management of irritable bowel syndrome (IBS) seem more transferential than biomedical:

> Key management issues in IBS include a positive clinical diagnosis, tests to exclude other diseases, and, if required, targeting drug therapy for the major symptoms. Reassurance, explanation, advice about possible precipitating factors, and exploration of psychological issues may be therapeutic. Follow-up to determine the response to treatment and to reinforce these general principles also appears to be of value. A 30-year historical cohort study suggested that a good doctor-patient relationship was linked to a marked reduction in subsequent visits to the

doctor. A placebo represents excellent therapy; the placebo response varied from 30% to 80% in short-term trials, and it may even increase with time. (2062)

Despite recognizing the role of the psyche in disturbances of the gut, the biomedical literature struggles to understand what kinds of relationships can be mapped between psyche and gut. The clinical and anecdotal data demand attention to affects, attachments, trauma, and chronic discontent, yet most commentators have difficulty integrating these concerns with the available biomedical data. One way or another, most of these commentators try to keep psychology at a distance from the gut.

For Talley (2001), psychological events (e.g., a good doctor-patient relationship) pertain to the "general management" of IBS. The focus of his paper is, seemingly, elsewhere, that is, on the treatment of IBS with drugs that regulate serotonin in the gut. IBS (hypersensitivity of the bowel) is one of the most prevalent of the functional gastrointestinal disorders (i.e., gut disorders with no identifiable biological basis), and functional disorders of the gut are more frequently encountered in the clinic than are organic diseases of the gut (Jones et al. 2000). Talley envisages that eventually the "pejorative" classification of IBS as a functional disorder will be discarded and IBS will come to be known as an organic bowel disease (perhaps with a genetic component). Once this has come to pass, the treatment of IBS can be more properly focused on the physiology of gut infections and inflammations and the drugs that can prevent or control these events.[11] What is pejorative about the terminology "functional" is the implication of psychological (hysterical) causality. To rescue IBS from a functional classification is to rescue its sufferers from the insinuation that this affliction (like Fraulein Elisabeth's muscular pain) is all in the head, and to return to the gut its properly enteric rather than psychological status. In other words, Talley considers psychological events to be peripheral to the task of isolating an etiology and treatment for IBS. Or perhaps more precisely, Talley considers psychological events to be metaconcerns ("general management") that are not legible or influential at the enterological level. For Talley, what happens in the gut is only secondarily or accidentally psychological.[12]

This flight from a psychological etiology (it's all in the head) is a common biomedical response to the treatment of functional gastrointestinal disorders (FGIDS). Woods et al. (1999), for example, recognize that "abdominal pain, diarrhea, nausea, altered food intake, and emesis [vomiting] can all be manifestations of emotional or traumatic stress" (118) and that the gut functions through localized nervous mechanisms in the gut wall. That is, they recognize both the importance of psychological events on the gut and the likelihood that ENS mechanisms play a prominent role in gut function.

However, they do not envisage that the neurology of the gut may also engender a psychology of the gut. For Woods et al., psychological events are at a distance from enterology; the psychology of the gut is governed by CNS (rather than ENS) innervation: "Findings that antidepressant medications relieve some FGID symptoms [are] evidence of disorder in the higher brain centers that influence the outflow of commands to the gut . . . The stress-related symptoms and behavioral changes (i.e., sleep disturbances, muscle tension, pain, altered diet, abnormal illness behavior) associated with FGIDS probably reflect subtle malfunctions in the brain circuits responsible for interactions of higher cognitive functions and central centers that determine outputs to the gastrointestinal tract, and not to psychiatric illness alone" (II8). These kinds of summarizing statements give the impression of a nervous system in which higher-order (cognitive) centers are the origin and locale of psychological events. Psychological events affect the gut, but they seem to be happening elsewhere (i.e., in the brain).

Time and again, researchers in the field of neurogastroenterology return to the CNS as the sole source of psychological influence, even as they advocate complex, multifactorial models of functional gut disorder. Drossman (1999), for example, claims that recent FGID research has shifted away from unidirectional models of psychosocial influence (e.g., stress) on the gut, and toward "a more integrated, biopsychosocial model of illness" (II1). He claims that a "reciprocal interaction of physiologic and psychosocial processes" underlies FGIDS (Drossman, Creed, Olden, Svedlund, Toner, and Whithead 1999, II25). This reciprocal interaction plays out along the "brain-gut axis," a loosely defined circuit that connects the ENS, spinal cord, and CNS (Wilhelmsen 2000). Interesting as such models seem, there is not yet enough conceptual attention being paid to the component parts of such an axis and to their interrelations (see chapter 1). In particular, the CNS still governs the way the psyche is understood. Psychological events are confined to the higher neurological centers and transported down to the gut. "Reciprocal interaction" turns out to be simply a movement back and forth from one end of the body to the other. What begins encouragingly as a model of heterogeneous "biopsychosocial" influence becomes unidirectional in precisely the way Drossman seems to want to avoid: "We emphasize a more integrative biopsychosocial understanding of these [FGID] symptoms as being generated by a combination of intestinal, motor, sensory, and CNS activity—the brain-gut axis. Thus, extrinsic (vision, smell, etc.) or enteroceptive (emotion, thought) information [has], by nature of [its] neural connections from higher centers, the capability to affect gastrointestinal sensation, motility, secretion, and inflammation" (1999, II3).

Although the brain-gut axis might provide a useful anatomical map of ENS-CNS connection, it is too simple in functional and psychological terms.

Nervous innervation doesn't loop through the gut, spinal cord, and brain like a car on a racing track. Nervous signals in the gut, for example, are dispersed through the anatomically extensive nervous networks that make up the enteric plexuses, where they are "amplified, weakened, or otherwise modulated" (Gershon 1998, 11). At various points in this putative brain-gut axis there are local eddies that collect, transform, dampen down, distribute, duplicate, and magnify the innervations they receive. These neurological assemblages form a series of "mini-brains"—sites of psychological intensity—that arrest and divert axial traffic. The notion of psychological action at a distance ("disorders in higher brain centers") misjudges the radically distributed and communicative nature of the body's nervous systems. That antidepressant medications relieve some FGID symptoms may be evidence not simply of CNS influence on the gut. This may also be evidence that medications have an antidepressant effect on the gut itself. It is not just the mind via the brain that is being revitalized by SSRI medication; the mindfulness particular to the gut is also being made more confident, flexible, resilient, and assertive.[13] That is, the ENS has its own neuropsychological profile: the various nervous plexuses in the gut form differentiated networks for mood, affect regulation, and attachment along with the networks for sensation and motility.

Many researchers using ENS data to rethink the treatment of FGIDs misconstrue the nature of psychological events. There is a tendency in the texts mentioned above to restrict psychological events to cognitive events and to hyperbolically equate psychological disequilibrium with psychiatric illness. But psychological events have a more diverse profile than simply being consciously available and under the governance of the will or conditioning regimes. Many psychological events are unconscious or innate or temperamental or affective; in fact, most psychological events are of this kind. Cognitions are simply the most accessible of our psychological capacities, and psychiatric illnesses are the disruptions most legible to a cognitively oriented epistemology. The vicissitudes of everyday disequilibria—insecurity, loss, embarrassment, fury, procrastination—demand a theory of the psyche that is more extensive and less attached to the primacy of rationality, self-control, good judgment, and sound appraisal. If the psychological landscape could be more broadly surveyed, if, for example, it could be seen to be composed of an innately affective nervous system, then psychological events could be more readily integrated into biomedical accounts of gut function.[14] The ongoing failure in Talley, Woods, and Drossman to instantiate psychology at the enterological level speaks to the strangely disembodied way in which scientific accounts of cognition have been generated, and to how the CNS has come to embody this type of cognition.[15]

Gershon (1998) struggles much more explicitly with this dilemma of psychology and the gut. Whereas Talley, Woods, and Drossman wish to move any psychological influence on the gut away from the gut itself to higher CNS centers, Gershon seems to want to rid the gut of as much psychological influence as possible—including the CNS: "When behaviors of the bowel that are essentially under enteric control are disturbed, it is by no means clear that the output of the enteric nervous system is aberrant *because the brain has made it so*. Since the brain in the head affects the second brain [i.e., the ENS], it is, of course, conceivable that a disturbed mind may transmit its problems to the enteric nervous system, thereby upsetting even the functions delegated to the second brain. There is nothing, however, to prevent the enteric nervous system itself from giving rise to enteric misbehavior, independently of any influence the second brain receives from the first" (177).

It is Gershon who gets more mileage than his colleagues out of the paucity of vagal connection between brain and bowel. The anatomical autonomy of the ENS from the CNS is such, Gershon hopes, that the ENS may be largely protected from psychological (i.e., CNS) influence. In time, the functional (i.e., psychological) aspects of gastrointestinal illness will be reformulated in more specifically enterological terms: "Today, functional bowel disease is a complex of symptoms lacking a link to pathology. Tomorrow, I am sure that list will vanish and be replaced by an assortment of evident disease entities. Crohn's disease was once a form of functional bowel disease, but it was removed from this fraternity when its pathology was discovered" (Gershon 1998, 187). Like Talley, Gershon hopes that neurogastroenterological research will eventually rid the gut of the impression of the psyche. In fact, he considers psychological theories of gut disorder to be "primitive" (177) and "supernatural" (178). At its most intense, this antipsychologism takes the form of anti-Freudianism: "When all else fails, invoke a psychoneurosis" (177). Wilhelmsen (2000) likewise mobilizes neurology to displace Freudianism: "In spite of many decades of research, there is no evidence that emotions can 'pile up' somewhere in the body and that psychological conflicts, if unresolved, are converted to somatic symptoms or diseases. On the contrary . . . unresolved mental conflicts lead to activation of the central nervous system . . . and of the autonomic systems" (IV5).

Contra Gershon and Wilhelmsen, I take Freudianism to have a uniquely vitalizing effect on contemporary understandings of the neurology of the gut. In its earliest form, psychoanalysis was working with the nervous body in ways that underscored the appetency of nervous and psychological systems for each other. In comparison to bloodless, gutless theories of cognition, psychoanalytic theories have a much greater affinity for neurological data. In the case of Frau Emmy, her transferential relations to Freud aren't simply in her head (or in her brain), they are in her gut. These relations are more strongly serotonergic, vagal, and mucosal than they are cognitive. Her gut responds directly to psychological duress ("I found Frau Emmy . . . lying in a profoundly depressed state and a very ungracious mood. She complained of having very violent gastric pains"), not simply because there is a relay of information from higher cortical centers, but more immediately because of the consanguinity of enterology and mood. An effective intervention into Frau Emmy's condition requires that this natural affinity of gut and psyche be respected. Freud comes to understand that he cannot remove her symptoms didactically or cognitively; he instead intervenes locally and psychologically on the skin, in relation to the muscles and glands and nerves and fear ("I then removed her gastric pains by stroking her a few times across the epigastrium").[16]

Freud's early texts struggle to explain nerves and stomach and fear and grief together. They remain exemplary texts for contemporary theories of the nervous system to the extent that they make the puzzle of neuropsychic relations explicit. The recognition that Freud's neurology is outmoded or that his psychological methods are underdeveloped is no doubt the easiest thing to say about these texts. What seems more important is that he attends to the transferential nature of the nerves. Freud's antiquated methods illustrate a consanguinity of nerves, psyche, and gut that even the most sophisticated of contemporary knowledges are still struggling to grasp.

Gut Depression

The ENS is in contact with a number of other nervous and biological systems, such that it is not possible to argue for its autonomy or independence in any radical way. Most researchers in the field struggle to adequately conceptualize the relation between the ENS and the CNS—that is, to reformulate old-fashioned notions of nervous system hierarchy in which the brain governs the periphery. They struggle all the more to understand the vicissitudes of the ENS-psyche interface. While acknowledging the clinical significance of depressive, stressful, anxious, or affective states on the gut, most researchers do not articulate these effects at the microbiological coalface: Are some inflammations depressive? Others angry? How do the enteric plexuses distribute not just action potentials, but also anxieties, frustrations, or grief?[17] I suggested in the previous section that the gut is in a natural alliance with psychological events, that there is something about the gut that makes it a particularly potent psychological organ. In this final section, I expand on this putative affinity of gut and mood, especially in relation to depression.

A psychologically barren ENS becomes implausible when we consider one noteworthy aspect of the gut: that it is one of the most important means by which the outside world connects with the body. Woods et al. (1999) under-stand this connection to the outside as something of a threat: "In its position in the colon, the mucosal immune system encounters one of the most contaminated of bodily interfaces with the outside world. The system is exposed daily to dietary antigens, bacteria, viruses, and toxins. Physical and chemical barriers at the epithelial interface do not exclude the large antigenic load in its entirety, causing the mucosal immune system to be chronically challenged" (II12). Gershon (1998) likens the gut to the skin: both form boundaries between self and world. In the case of the gut, this boundary allows the outside world to pass through us: "The space enclosed within the wall of the bowel, its *lumen*, is part of the outside world. The open tube that begins at the mouth ends at the anus. Paradoxical as it may seem, the gut is a tunnel that permits the exterior to run right through us. Whatever is in the lumen of the gut is thus actually outside of our bodies" (84). Charles Darwin (1859) made a similar observation in relation to worms: he notes that the fertile soil on the surface of the earth has passed through the alimentary canal of worms many times over (see chapter 5). For Darwin, a crucial part of the organic world is the product of an internal biological environment. Commenting on the gut's heterogeneous, invertebrate origins, Darwin notes that the gut seems particularly predisposed to the inversion of inside and out: "Numerous cases could be given amongst the lower animals of the same organ performing at the same time wholly distinct functions; thus the ali-mentary canal respires, digests, and excretes in the larva of the dragon-fly and in the fish Cobites. In the Hydra, the animal may be turned inside out, and the exterior surface will then digest and the stomach will respire" (155). For an internal organ the gut has a remarkably intimate connection to the outside.

What the outside world engenders in the psychological sphere is relations to others, and through this the development of the self. It is the dynamics of intersubjective relations that allow the self to emerge and stabilize. These relations to others are psychologically generative only to the extent that they are internalized (ingested, absorbed, excreted).[18] Even in psychodynamic spheres, however, the internalization of relations with others tends to be discussed mainly in ideational terms. As psychoanalysis has developed, and as drive theory becomes less influential, the biology of transference (how it plays out inside bodies and between bodies) has become less evident. At the same time, there has been increasing psychoanalytic interest in the role of the brain in the integration of experience of others. Notwithstanding the scope of these new psychoanalytic-neurological syntheses (e.g., Schore 1999), it is my concern that the ideational focus of these accounts coupled with their enthusiasm for the CNS reinforces the notion that the internaliza-tion of good relations to others and the damaging effects of traumatizing or destructive relations to others are events that take place in the head (and are only secondarily related to the body). The broader biology of how relations to others are internalized still requires elucidation, and such an elucidation demands an understanding of psychic action embodied beyond the CNS. To the extent that the gut is attuned to the outside world, it is a vital organ in the maintenance of relations to others.

Depression is a breakdown in relations to others. The sustaining effects of others have been removed, either chronically or suddenly, and the self is unable to hold itself together, disintegrating into either an affectless immobilization or agitation (or sometimes, paradoxically, both). Speaking psychodynamically, depression is a chronic, inflexible response to the loss of another. The self becomes depleted in the face of isolation and injury and is unable to access others (either internally or in the world). The biochemical thesis of depression is concerned with a different kind of depletion: a drop in neurotransmitter levels in CNS synapses. Despite the differences between these models, they both understand breakdowns in the gut to be central to the etiology of depression. From his earliest investigations, Freud was aware of the close links between digestion and psychology, especially food and melancholia. In an early draft to Fliess, where he attempts a neurological explanation of melancholia, Freud argues that "the famous anorexia nervosa of young girls" (1895a, 200) is the nutritional parallel of melancholia. Where the melancholic loses libidinal attachment, the anorexic loses her hunger: "she has no appetite" (200).[19] In contemporary psychiatric contexts, disruptions to appetite are used to diagnose mood disorders, especially depression. A major depressive episode entails alteration of mood and "at least four additional symptoms drawn from a list that includes changes in appetite or weight" (American Psychiatric Association 1994, 320). It is typical that appetite is reduced in depression, and patients may feel, like Frau Emmy, that "they have to force themselves to eat" (321).

Maybe ingestion and digestion aren't just metaphors for internalization; perhaps they are "actual" mechanisms for relating to others. That is, perhaps gut pathology doesn't stand in for ideational disruption, but is another form of perturbed relations to others—a form that is enacted enterologically. The large stocks of serotonin in the gut, the morphological similarities between gut neurons and brain neurons, and the clearly psychological character of gut function all suggest that it is not just ideation that is disrupted in depression; it is also the gut. I am arguing that psychodynamic and neuroenterological data could be used to build a schema of depression in which the failure to eat doesn't represent a breakdown of connection to others, but is seen as a direct interruption to the process of remaining connected to others. The struggle to eat (or to stop eating) when depressed is a struggle to mediate difficult, attenuated, or lost relations to others and to the outside world. The associated gastrointestinal difficulties—bloatedness, nausea, vomiting, constipation, diarrhea—are modes of distress enacted enterologically.

Enterological breakdown is a consistent theme in Andrew Solomon's (1998, 2001) account of his episodes of major depression. As he became emotionally fragile and less able to sleep, he also "began eating irregularly, seldom feeling hungry" (1998, 46), and he became gripped by fear: "I lay in bed, not sleeping and hugging my pillow for comfort. Two weeks later—the day before my thirty-first birthday—I left the house once, to buy groceries; petrified for no reason, I suddenly lost bowel control and soiled myself. I ran home, shaking, and went to bed, but I did not sleep, and could not get up the following day" (46).

His condition worsens, and he feels as though he has "a physical need, of impossible urgency and discomfort, from which there was no release—as though I were constantly vomiting but had no mouth" (48). As he begins to recover from his first depressive breakdown, he experiences a violent regression in both his mood and his gut. Having recovered sufficiently to go to the movies with a friend, he returns home and becomes distressed:

> When I came home, I felt a return of panic, and a sadness of dinosaur proportions. I went into the bathroom and threw up repeatedly, as though my acute understanding of my loneliness were a virus in my system. I thought that I would die alone, and that there was no good reason to stay alive, and I thought that the normal and real world in which I had grown up, and in which I believed that other people lived, would never open itself up to receive me. And as these revelations burst into my head like shots, I retched on the bathroom floor, and the acid rode up the length of my esophagus, and when I tried to catch my breath, I inhaled my own bile. I had been eating big meals to try to put weight back on, and I felt as though all of them were coming back up, as though my stomach were going to turn itself inside out and hang limp in the toilet. (2001, 67)

Like Darwin's Hydra, Solomon's gut is turning itself inside out, unsure whether to digest or respire ("when I tried to catch my breath, I inhaled my own bile"), unsure how to situate itself in relation to the rest of the body and to the world. His diminished capacity to be with others is not being played out in his head and then transferred to the gut; the gut itself is unable to take in the world, to let others pass through him and be absorbed.

The transferential nature of Solomon's enteric nervous system is made evident by the responsiveness of his gut to both loneliness and kindness. His father played an important role in his recovery from this episode of breakdown; eating with his father became emblematic of both the depressive collapse and its remedy: "At dinner, I would feel unable to eat, but I could get up and sit in the dining room with my father, who canceled all other plans to be with me. My father nodded, implacably assured me that it would pass, and tried to make me eat. He cut up my food. I told him not to feed me, that I wasn't five, but when I was defeated by the difficulty of getting a piece of lamb chop on my fork, he would do it for me. All the while, he would remember feeding me when I was a tiny child, and he would make me promise, jesting, to cut up his lamb chops when he was old and had lost his teeth" (2001, 54).

Largely unable to feel or connect with others, Solomon is able to enter into a relation of reciprocated care with his father through the gut. At this moment, the gut has become Solomon's most viable, most dexterous means of accessing others. Where Freud was able to intervene in Frau Emmy's gastric depression with hypnosis and stroking of the abdomen, Solomon's father has worked more intersubjectively on the inside of the gut (we will have fed each other) to reestablish his son's relations to the world and to lift the depression that threatens to kill him.

Solomon's recovery from depression was facilitated not just by his gastric relation to his father, but also by the use of SSRI antidepressants and psychotherapy. It is this cohabitation of mood and parent and therapist and serotonin and food that seems to elude both psychoanalytic and neurogastroenterological accounts of gut disorder. How can a father's love become changes in enteric pathways? What kinds of ontologies are needed to understand how serotonergic systems and systems of parental care both reside in the gut? It has been the argument of this chapter that both neurogastroenterology and psychoanalysis have become too interested in the CNS and the head as the focus of their treatment regimes. The nervous system extends well beyond the skull, and as it so travels through the body it takes the psyche with it. The transferential nature of the nervous system (i.e., its obligatory relations to other systems: biochemical, psychological, enterological) has yet to be grasped in either psychoanalytic or gastroenterological frameworks.

Chapter 4 returns to Darwin to explore the kinds of (trembling, blushing) psychosomatic relations that the peripheral nervous system generates. Before that, chapter 3 examines the brain, specifically the hypothalamus, to see how the CNS itself could be more divergently mapped.

· · · · · · · ·   3

· · · · · · · ·   Hypothalamic Preference: LeVay's Study

of Sexual Orientation

· · · · · · · ·   The discovery that a nucleus differs in size between heterosexual and homosexual men illustrates that sexual orientation in humans is amenable to study at the biological level, and this discovery opens the door to studies of
neurotransmitters or receptors that might be involved in regulating this aspect of
personality.[1] Further interpretation of the results of this study must be considered
speculative. —LeVay 1991

Simon LeVay's caveat that interpretation of his data should be delimited has
been widely disregarded. In the wake of his 1991 report in *Science* there has
been little in the way of new data on the neurotransmitters and receptors
that may be involved in regulating sexuality, and to date there has been no
published replication of LeVay's key findings.[2] There has, however, been
much in the way of further interpretation of his report by academic, scientific, political, legal, and media commentators.[3]
  For a study that is reliant on simple symmetrical axes of analysis (hetero
vs. homo; male-typical vs. female-typical), LeVay's article has incited a curiously variant set of responses: gay activists who welcome the political implications of a biologically conferred homosexuality (Pillard in Stein 1993),
feminist scientists who doubt the robustness of LeVay's data (Fausto-Sterling
1992), critics who broach the antihomophobic possibilities of biological
research into sexuality while maintaining reservations about the particularities of LeVay's study (Rosario 1997; Stein 1999), scientists who integrate
LeVay's results into a contentious body of research on the causes of homosexuality (Swaab, Zhou, Fodor, and Hofman 1997), cultural critics who find
LeVay's conceptualization of sexuality and sexual identity too static (Garber

1995; Terry 2000), psychologists who argue that LeVay's work could be read as latent poststructuralist genealogy (Gordo-López and Cleminson 1999), a psychologist who argues that LeVay's work is a conventional reiteration of heterosexist norms (Hegarty 1997), a philosopher who compares LeVay to Monique Wittig (Zita 1998), a legal theorist who warns against the use of biological theories of sexual orientation in pro-gay litigation (Halley 1994), and a neuroscientific colleague who was harshly critical of LeVay's article—arguing that it should not have been published—but who later replicated a key finding of that study (Byne 1995; Byne et al. 2000).

Within the humanities-bound literature there has been extensive commentary on the ways LeVay's original study is limited both methodologically and conceptually. For example, it has been argued that the medical records of postmortem individuals contain insufficient data to reliably allocate those individuals to different categories of sexual identity, that LeVay's use of the categories heterosexual and homosexual is modeled on outdated notions of sexual identity, that the brains of many of the subjects may have been modified by complications from AIDS, that LeVay conflates male homosexuality with femininity, that the sample size is too small for reliable comparisons between groups to be made, that LeVay's hypothesis can be supported only when data from the brains of homosexual women are included in the comparative schema, and that LeVay's assertion that studies of rodent and primate sexuality offer useful behavioral and neurological homologies for humans is not valid.[4]

This chapter does not offer more in the way of this kind of commentary. Nor am I concerned with the debates about the nature and nurture of homosexuality that have been reignited by LeVay's report and by genetic studies of homosexuality published about the same time (Bailey and Pillard 1991; Hamer, Hu, Magnuson, Hu, and Pattatucci 1993; LeVay and Hamer 1994). Instead, this chapter offers some speculations about the kind of neurological substance that is revealed in LeVay's study. By paying close attention to the specifics of LeVay's data, I hope to show one way that neurological substrate and sexuality can be allied. I clarify the relation between, on the one hand, the inertly dimorphic forms of sexuality that LeVay's methodology uses and, on the other hand, the exceptional (distributed) neurological and sexual forms in his data. It has been typical in commentaries on the 1991 study that only one of these patterns is respected. Pro-LeVay commentators tend to focus on the dimorphic distribution of his data and thus endorse simplistic notions of homosexuality and heterosexuality. Anti-LeVay commentators attempt to refute the validity of this dimorphic pattern by discussing the ways sexualities breach the confines of hetero/homo definition. This chapter makes a case that this analytic choice (dimorphic vs. distributed) obscures a more useful reading of the data. I argue that it is the relationship between dimorphic and distributed forms that is most instructive in LeVay's study.

This analysis of the dimorphic (n=2) and the divergent (n>2) serves as a template for examining the convergence of brain and sexuality. I leave to one side an analysis of what LeVay's data might be able to tell us about sexuality; by and large, LeVay presumes a conventional theory of gender-bound sexuality.[5] I am more interested in how this study of sexuality and the brain might reorganize our expectations about the character of neurology; specifically, how the reticulation of the hypothalamus by a dimorphic sexuality may provide insight into the nature of neurological substrata.

I recruit "reticulation" as a way of elucidating the relationship between dimorphic articulations (homo/hetero; large/small) on the one hand and the circuitry of neurological structures and the exceptionality of outlying data on the other. "Reticulate, v. 1. To divide or mark in such a way as to resemble [a] network. 2. To divide so as to form a network, or something having that appearance" (OED).[6] Rather than argue that there is an interpretive choice (or a political imperative) to favor dissemination over dimorphism, I suggest that these two kinds of neurological forms are in a reticulated relationship, wherein dimorphic divisions are irreducibly, agonistically, generatively conjoined with networks of divergence.

A Difference in Hypothalamic Structure
in Heterosexual and Homosexual Men

First of all, and as a way of introducing some particularity to the discussion of LeVay's data about the hypothalamus and sexual orientation, let's consider the empirical antecedents, method, and outcomes of the 1991 study.

LeVay drew on two sets of empirical evidence to establish his hypothesis about the hypothalamus and sexuality. First, animal studies suggested that the medial zone of the anterior hypothalamus is implicated in what the literature nominates as "male-typical" sexual behavior (i.e., mounting). Second, one study indicated that lesions to this area impaired heterosexual behavior but did not eliminate sexual drive per se. Lesions to the medial preoptic anterior hypothalamus in male rhesus monkeys resulted in decreased frequency of sexual contact with female monkeys (measured as levels of manual contact, mounting, intromission, and ejaculation); however, there was no decrease in the frequency of masturbation (Slimp, Hart, and Goy 1978).[7] These data have been used to argue that this part of the hypothalamus controls heterosexuality, but not sexual drive in general.

Following on from this research, LeVay contended that an area in the human hypothalamus homologous to this area in other animals may be involved in regulating sexual behavior in men and women. Importantly for

LeVay, these homologous nuclei in the human hypothalamus had already been reported to be significantly larger in men than in women (Allen, Hines, Shryne, and Gorski 1989). Moreover, this dimorphism in size had been interpreted as evidence that these nuclei may contribute to functional differences not only between men and women, but also between individuals of different sexual orientation: "Morphological analysis of the brains from humans with different sexual orientations and identities . . . may lead to further deductions concerning the possible influences of sex hormones on the structure and function of the human brain" (Allen et al. 1989, 504).[8] LeVay took up Allen et al.'s suggestion, but inverted the primacy accorded to gender in their study. He hypothesized that the reported dimorphism in certain hypothalamic nuclei in humans may be primarily related not to gender differences, but to differences in sexual orientation: "Specifically, I hypothesized that INAH [interstitial nuclei of the anterior hypothalamus] 2 or INAH 3 is large in individuals sexually oriented towards women (heterosexual men and homosexual women) and small in individuals sexually oriented toward men (heterosexual women and homosexual men)" (1991, 1035).

To test this hypothesis, LeVay measured the volume of the four hypothalamic nuclei that Allen et al. had investigated. They had named these "previously undescribed cell groups" (1989, 497) the interstitial nuclei of the anterior hypothalamus: INAH 1, 2, 3, 4. LeVay obtained brain tissue from forty-one subjects: nineteen homosexual men (their homosexuality was noted in their medical records), sixteen (presumed) heterosexual men, and six (presumed) heterosexual women.[9] The brain tissue was chemically fixed, the area containing the hypothalamic nuclei was dissected, and sliced sections were mounted on slides and stained. Measurement of the nuclei was undertaken by projecting magnifications of each section of tissue onto paper so that the nucleus is clearly visible, and then tracing an outline around that structure: "The outline of each nucleus was drawn as the shortest line that included every cell of the type characteristic for that nucleus, regardless of cell density . . . the volume of each nucleus was calculated as the summed area of the serial outlines multiplied by the section thickness" (LeVay 1991, 1035).[10]

LeVay's 1991 report has two micrographs that illustrate the differences in the volume of these nuclei. The micrograph of INAH 3 from a heterosexual man shows a well-defined, densely packed area; the micrograph of INAH 3 from a homosexual man, on the other hand, "is poorly recognizable as a distinct nucleus, but scattered cells similar to those constituting the nucleus in the heterosexual men were found" (1035). Indeed, "in most of the homosexual men (and most of the women) the nucleus was represented by only scattered cells" (1036).

Statistical analysis of the differences in volume among the nuclei of the women, heterosexual men, and homosexual men showed that, on average, INAH 3 was "more than twice as large in heterosexual men . . . as in the homosexual men" and that "there was a similar difference between the heterosexual men and the women" (LeVay 1991, 1035). There were no significant differences in the other nuclei studied (INAH 1, 2, 4). From these data LeVay claims some tentative support for the hypothesis that INAH 3 is dimorphic in relation to sexual orientation rather than in relation to gender; that is, small in those individuals, men or women, sexually oriented to men and large in those individuals, men or women, sexually oriented to women. He is unable to fully support such a conclusion as he requires data from the brains of lesbians to complete the comparative schema. Nonetheless, the established anatomical dimorphism is presumed to entail a functional dimorphism of INAH 3, and so imply that, at least in men, "sexual orientation has a biological substrate" (1034).

Reticulating Neurology

In the final paragraphs of the 1991 report, LeVay discussed a number of factors that may contaminate his data: the difficulty in actually defining which cells belonged to a nucleus, the absence of brain tissue from homosexual women, the effects of AIDS and AIDS-related conditions on the volume of the nuclei in some of his subjects, the possibility that individuals who have died from AIDS are an unrepresentative sample of the male homosexual population, and the limitations that postmortem medical records place on representing "the diversity of sexual behavior that undoubtedly exists within the homosexual and heterosexual populations" (1036).

These concerns have been exploited in many critical commentaries, although perhaps they represent no more than the usual limitations that any empirical study of this kind has to endure. It is LeVay's final reservation that strikes me as more engaging, as it foregrounds the complexity in his data and the dynamic organization of neurological substrate: "The existence of 'exceptions' in the present sample (that is, presumed heterosexual men with small INAH 3 nuclei, and homosexual men with large ones) hints at the possibility that sexual orientation, although an important variable, may not be the sole determinant of INAH 3 size" (1036).

Leaving aside the question of what determines the size of INAH 3 (as there just are not sufficient data here or in the literature generally to adjudicate on this matter), the existence of "exceptions" in the sample is important. The INAH 3 data show a fair degree of variation. The second largest INAH 3 was in a homosexual man (when the trend was for INAH 3 in homosexual men to be small); the volumes of the three smallest nuclei in the heterosexual men closely matched those of the homosexual men (whereas most of the nuclei from heterosexual men were significantly larger than the nuclei of homosexual men); and two of the six female nuclei were similar in volume to the heterosexual men's (though, as a group, the female nuclei were similar in size to the smaller nuclei of homosexual men; see figure 2). LeVay offers the suggestion that these exceptions may be due to "technical shortcomings or to misassignment of subjects to their subject groups" (1036). However, his prior recognition of "the diversity of sexual behavior that undoubtedly exists within the homosexual and heterosexual populations" preempts any expectation that subjects will fall naturally into two discretely contained categories. And herein lies the interpretive crux of LeVay's study: how to account for a body of data that both clusters in a statistically significant dimorphic pattern and manifests exceptional, outlying measurements that directly contradict this pattern.

The preference for analyzing data in terms of dimorphisms was well established in the neurobiological literature prior to LeVay's study. Sexual dimorphisms—the existence of anatomical and functional differences between male and female brains—had been alleged for over 150 years (Fausto-Sterling 2000). In the years prior to LeVay's study there had been increasing interest in male/female differences in various hypothalamic nuclei (Swaab, Chung, Kruijver, Hofman, and Ishunina 2001; Swaab, Gooren, and Hofman 1992).[11] LeVay conscripts this conceptual framework into his study on sexual orientation, hypothesizing that a hetero/homo dimorphism will also be evident in the hypothalamus. I am interested in engaging this conceptual proclivity for dimorphisms (n=2) a little further—to see what dimorphic structures might generate in relation to neurology and sexuality. It is true enough that n=2 has often been the very worst place to start and end interpretation about sexual difference and differences in sexual orientation. But it is not therefore a place to be avoided altogether: a comprehensive understanding of sexual differentiation needn't require the abandonment of this remarkably powerful figuration.[12] My challenge in relation to LeVay's data is not to recite the heteronormative aspects of n=2, but to explore how the simplicity of a dimorphic pattern contributes to the elaborations, refractions, and de-evolutions of neurological substance.

Standard statistical interpretation guarantees that the dimorphic pattern predominates over the outlying data. Exceptional data require explanation, but they do not disrupt the robustness of the main division in nucleic volume in the sample. By all regular scientific and statistical conventions, LeVay's data manifest a dimorphic division in the size of INAH 3.[13] The conventions of critical, humanities-based commentary, on the other hand, dispute this statistical interpretation. For these commentators, sexuality is constituted according to a more distributed logic; sexualities are not ordered

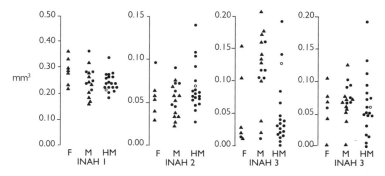

Figure 2. Volumes of interstitial nuclei of the anterior hypothalamus (INAH) 1, 2, 3, 4. Reprinted with permission from Simon LeVay, "A difference in hypothalamic structure between heterosexual and homosexual men," *Science* 253: 1036. Copyright 1991 American Association for the Advancement of Science.

into two symmetrical groupings (hetero/homo). Outlying data are not evidence of technical slips or methodological aberrations, they are part of the natural diversity of human sexualities. In this vein, Janet Halley (1994) has been particularly articulate:

> LeVay's method excludes from consideration the complex social patterns of identity profession and ascription, the refracting layers of representation in which the image of sexual orientation is managed, groomed, appropriated, negotiated, and captured. He reduced this complexity to a single characteristic: essential sexual orientation lodged neatly within the atomized individual who has died.
>
> This exclusion of the social and representational aspects of sexual orientation identity makes LeVay's handling of his bipolar categories, homosexual and heterosexual, almost startlingly crude . . . Whatever the ultimate resolution of those debates about experimental technique, LeVay's deployment of his categories remains open to cultural criticism for ignoring the complexity of his subject. By making his heterosexual class a universal default, LeVay insists that all persons are indeed located in one of his two classifications. As a matter of theoretical assumption, he eliminates the possibility of a person with a sexuality neither heterosexual nor homosexual . . . LeVay's error was more grave than simply misclassifying some subjects who are "really" heterosexual as homosexual, or vice versa. He has changed the nature of his categories from the merely lexical to the ontological. His method forced these categories to describe and conclude the entire range of human possibility—to constitute us, no matter who we are and what we do or feel. (536–537)

For Halley, the dimorphic pattern in LeVay's data misrepresents the range of human possibility; human sexualities manifest a complexity that is not reducible to the bipolar categories hetero/homo. Halley's cultural orientation directly refutes the statistically based claim that a reliable dimorphic difference exists in the data. In a manner that is exemplary of the humanities-bound commentaries on the LeVay study, Halley annuls the dimorphic pattern in the data in favor of a more distributed organization. Jennifer Terry (2000) notes that researchers like LeVay rely too much on animal models of gender-typical sexual behavior (mounting and lordosis): "Assuming that gender typicality is the same across species allows researchers to ignore or misunderstand variance among individual animals and across species. This is precisely what happens in much of the research on human sexuality and sexual orientation that relies on the use of rodents" (161). Variance is lost or misrepresented when a dimorphic approach to sexual behavior (mounting and lordosis) is enacted. Timothy Murphy's (1997) commentary on the outlying data in LeVay's study reaffirms this inclination for variation. He emphasizes general differentiation over dimorphic difference: "There is no INAH 3 size at which sexual orientation divides neatly into homosexual and heterosexual categories, with the single bisexual man in the study straddling a dividing point between the two. Sizes of INAH 3 range, for gay men and straight men alike, over almost the entire gamut possible for that nucleus" (28). For Murphy, the statistically authorized dimorphic pattern is a ruse: there is no "two," there is in fact "almost the entire gamut." Nucleic volumes are not seen to "divide" but rather to "range" across a continuum of possible sizes. For Murphy, Halley, Terry, and many other critics of LeVay's work, the logic of the range is offered in order to replace or invalidate the logic of the divide. That is, the pattern of dimorphic division is repudiated as an interpretive possibility in favor of an interpretation of more divergent sexual forms.

The analyses that Halley, Terry, and Murphy construct are on target: clearly, LeVay gives no attention to the originary and constitutive nature of variation in sexual orientation. As Halley notes, dimorphism is a conceptual a priori for this research: it is assumed (male-typical, female-typical) rather than demonstrated. My comments are not intended to contest the general validity of the critiques offered by Halley, Terry, or Murphy. Nonetheless, I would like to suggest that LeVay's data might be more usefully interpreted according to an axis askew to both these critical concerns and the conventional statistical claims. What LeVay's data show is neither two discretely sexualized nuclei nor an aimless pattern of nucleic volumes. Rather, the data demonstrate a reticulating pattern, a coimplication of the disseminated (ranging) with the dimorphic (divided). In this reticulating structure neither of these patterns governs the field of neurological possibilities to the exclusion of the other. Instead, the data invite another, more difficult, interpretive challenge: to envisage how dimorphic patterns might relate to, be implicated in, arrest and cleave, but also be partially generative of, more distributed organizations.

In a set of literatures that is preoccupied with binarized concerns (either in scientific attempts to deploy crudely dyadic forms of sexuality or in critical attempts to definitively disrupt any form that might risk a familiarity with binarization), this reticulation of dimorphism with differentiation is an important point of departure: How does a simple division—large/small—participate in an expansive field of neurological and sexual ontologies? Is a dimorphic analytic axis simply an error, a failure to accommodate difference, or does it offer a particular approach to the notion of (sexual and neurological) difference that, though rudimentary, is nonetheless generative? The argument following on from here presumes that a nontrivial distinction can be made between a dimorphism (the division into two forms, e.g., large/small) and a binary (wherein there is less a cleaving into two forms than an ordering according to one form and its supplement, e.g., man/woman, human/technology, speech/writing). Hetero/homo distinctions are commonly ordered according to binarized concerns, but their alliance in LeVay with a dimorphic difference (large/small) suggests another manner in which the couplet homo/hetero may be instantiated. And rather than simply obliterating binarization, this dimorphic pattern brings the awkward, insistent, constitutively inconstant effects of binarization to the fore.

In this regard, the work of Eve Kosofsky Sedgwick has been particularly illuminating. Her readings of homo/heterosexual definition understand the dual logic of its "potent incoherences" (1990, 2). These readings document how the instability of homo/hetero as either a binarized or dimorphic coupling is precisely the source of—rather than the obstacle to—its generative power.[14] Moreover, Sedgwick's mobilization of queer has been singularly effective for its ability to account for how any queer (disseminated) articulation has a close and vital relation to the cleaving nature of homo/hetero organization. In a preamble on the term queer, Sedgwick notes, "Given the historical and contemporary force of the prohibitions against *every* same-sex sexual expression, for anyone to disavow those meanings, or to displace them from [queer's] definitional center, would be to dematerialize any possibility of queerness itself" (1993, 8). That is, the couplet homo/hetero stands in a reticulating relation to queer; the dimorphic and binarized instantiations of homosexuality and heterosexuality are not an impediment to queer materializations, but rather are peculiarly incoherent, peculiarly potent mechanisms of sexual generativity as such.

I am also guided by Sedgwick's petition for "a political vision of difference that might resist both binary homogenization and infinitizing trivialization" (Sedgwick and Frank 1995, 15). What gives Sedgwick and Frank's analysis particular purchase is their recognition that biology and biologism are an indispensable part of this vision. Recounting the instinctive resistance provoked in humanities-trained commentators by the di- or polymorphic essentialisms of biological explanation, Sedgwick and Frank note, "The resistance occurs because there seems to be some strong adhesion between the specification 'finitely many (n>2) values' and that conversation-stopping word, innate . . . Somehow it's hard to hold on to the concept of eight or thirteen (and yet not infinite) different kinds of—of anything important— without having a biological model somewhere in the vicinity. The adhesion may well be a historical development, as though some momentum of modernity . . . has so evacuated the conceptual space between two and infinity that it may require the inertial friction of a biologism to even suggest the possibility of reinhabiting that space" (15).

In relation to LeVay's study, the conceptual space I am attempting to reinhabit is one where the possibility of a dimorphic pattern (n=2) isn't obliterated by an imperative for de-binarized organization. That is, I am attempting to take seriously the impact—generative and degenerative—of dimorphic ontologies.

To put this another way, heterogeneity isn't simply the opposite (or negation) of a dimorphic pattern. The relationship between dimorphism and its others is more, well, heterogeneous than simple contrariety. Michael Fortun's (2003) work on genomics provides one method for thinking about the relationship of dimorphic and distributed forms—the chiasmus: "One of its operations in rhetoric is to join and distinguish, combine and reverse two terms. The chiasmus marks a folding into each other that, like any of a number of M. C. Escher prints, never settles down into a *first this, then that* image, statement, or concept. Rhetorically, the chiasmus marks the spot where two distinct concepts can't be distinguished from each other, but feed off each other, send silent coded messages between themselves, and set possibilities in motion: not the smooth and simple interaction between distinct entities (nature and nurture, to cite just one familiar example), but the inescapably volatile and generative operations of an aporia" (23).

Fortun literalizes the chiasmus in the notation χ (chi), and uses it as a central analytic tool in examining how genomics, technoscience, governmentality, economics, and speculation have crossbred during the trading of Icelandic genetic and genealogical information. Referring to his neologism lavaχland, Fortun says: "The χ in lavaχland marks the fissure out of which emerges both flowing lava and solid land. The figure marks the spot of volatility and speculation. It marks the place where lava and land are joined, in sameness while separated, in difference . . . It marks an *and*—lava and land—although it would be better to say that the χ marks the not—not lava, not land" (2001, 23).

Fortun's analysis is organized according to a series of chiasmatic formulations (deconstructionχbiology; geneχome; epistemologyχstock options; maniaχfundamentals; open futureχsafe harbor; promisingχgenomics; presumedχconsent; speculationχspeculation), and for each of these paired formulations, he offers a diagram of "irreducible complexities" (8). What the chiasmus delivers in this context is a means for diagramming complexity ($n>2$: "the massive amounts of genetic and other information now routinely pouring out of corporate, university, and government labs," 9) within a bilateral structure (aχb). This linking of complexity to the classical simplicity of a pair provides a powerful model for those of us working under threat of being analytically underwhelmed by formulations of difference where $n=2$ and analytically overwhelmed by the explosion of data, theories, and cross-disciplinary affiliations that characterize the contemporary scientific scene.

So too with LeVay. The patterns in his data, and the ontological organizations that they attempt to delineate, don't offer up an interpretive or political choice of either divided structurations or eccentric distributions. The data suggest a more complex structuration of rudimentary divisions and their vicissitudes: dimorphismχdivergence. This reticulating-chiasmatic configuration is not simply a continuum in which dimorphic and disseminating forms benignly cohabit (a bell curve of standard data and their deviations). What is interesting in the data is neither the demonstration of a clear distinction of hetero/homo differences (as LeVay would hope) nor the demonstration of exhaustively debinarized sexualities (as many of LeVay's critics have hoped), but rather the more confounding, less readily identifiable reticulation of conventionalized and exceptional neurological constitutions.

Hypothalamic Preference

My foregoing interest in the interpretations of pattern in LeVay's data is an attempt to approach the reticulating nature of neurological material. By containing my reflections to the substrate of neurology (that is, without taking immediate interpretive recourse to cultural, social, psychological, or representational contingencies), I hope to amplify neurology's natural intricacies.

The mammalian brain is a reticulating structure. Its most obvious morphological feature—the division into two cerebral hemispheres—cohabits with a divergent array of synaptic connections, neural pathways, functional and histological differentiations, and biochemical communications. If we consider simply the anatomy of neuronal connections, this complexity is almost beyond comprehension: by one estimation (Edelman 1992), there are around 10 billion neurons in the cortex alone, and each of these neurons has between 1,000 and 10,000 synaptic connections from other neurons. There are, then, about 1 trillion connections in the cortex; a sample of tissue the size of a match head contains around a billion connections. Edelman notes that "if we consider how connections might be variously combined, the number would be hyperastronomical—on the order of ten followed by millions of zeros. (There are about ten followed by eighty zeros' worth of positively charged particles in the whole known universe!)" (17).

Yet, at the same time, the brain is radically underconnected: neurons don't just connect anywhere, or at a great distance—their connections are typically made within locally defined functional and anatomical constraints. So while the anatomy of neuronal connections suggests an almost boundless functional capacity, it is also the case that there are constraints in terms of which neurons can participate in what functions. The visual areas of the brain, for example, have an architectural structure quite different from that of subcortical regions such as the hypothalamus, and in a rudimentary way, the cortex itself is divided into areas of functional specialization: motor cortex, association cortex, visual cortex, and so on. Much of the popular commentary on the brain is an attempt to negotiate one side or other of this reticulating puzzle: the brain is seen as either one of the most complex structures in the universe, or as an organ delimitable to simple, localized constraints.

The hypothalamus also instantiates this reticulating entanglement of symmetrical, localized, and disseminating organizations. The hypothalamus is a subcortical structure in the vertebrate forebrain that contains a number of nucleic foci. The nuclei of the hypothalamus are thought to control a number of different activities, many of which are homeostatic. The hypothalamus

> integrates the autonomic nervous system, with centers for sympathetic and parasympathetic control; receives impulses from the viscera. Ideally situated to act as an integration center for the endocrine and nervous systems, secreting various releasing factors into the pituitary portal system and neurosecretions into the posterior pituitary . . . Contains control centers for feeding and satiety—the latter inhibiting the former after feeding. In higher vertebrates, is a center for aggressive emotions and feelings and for psychosomatic effects. Contains a thirst center responding to extracellular fluid volume; helps regulate sleeping and waking patterns; monitors blood pH and concentration and, in homeotherms, body temperature. (Thain and Hickman 1996, 319)

At the same time, however, this functional heterogeneity is housed in symmetrical form: the hypothalamus is divided into left and right halves. Each nucleus within the hypothalamus is duplicated on the right and left, although there are no known functional or anatomical differences between the nuclei.[15] And although the hypothalamus is widely connected biochemically to the cortex and to other organs (e.g., the pituitary gland, and through it to the gonads), most of the information that the hypothalamus receives comes from itself (LeVay, 1993).

This relationality between simple, symmetrical forms and widely dispersing circuits is precisely what needs to be excavated from LeVay's 1991 data. The injection of a dimorphic sexuality into this field need not have the effect of arresting divergent neurological pathways. Although LeVay's transmogrification of sexual orientation into nucleic volume appears to be a hopelessly reductive gesture, the deployment of neurologically dimorphic forms need not in itself enact reductionism. If the brain does, in places, coalesce into symmetrical and localized organizations, it does so only within a wider circuitry that reticulates this localizing symmetry. Likewise, these circuits are themselves constituted through an intimate adhesion to localized dimorphisms. As I have attempted to argue, dimorphic, symmetrical forms are not necessarily degenerate, reductive, or inflexible, but may be generative constituents of overall neurological structure and function.

LeVay's study opens up at least two avenues for approaching the conjunction of neurology and sexuality. First, it allows the embodiment of sexual preference to be instantiated neurologically. It is parochial to expect that sexualities circulate only in nonbiological realms, that they could be contained to cultural domains, or that they could be arrested at the cell membrane or synaptic gap. If sexuality is sequestered within nonbiological organizations (culture, economics, semiosis), then the communicability of sexuality and the possibilities for perversion have been considerably diminished. Second (and following on from this first point), LeVay's insistence on the intimacy of INAH and sexuality opens sexuality up to a range of hypothalamic possibilities. It canvases the possible links between sexuality and, for example, body temperature, appetite, and circadian rhythms in ways that promise perverse and disseminated sexual forms. Not surprisingly, perhaps, LeVay has ruled out such a divergent biological substrate for sexuality. At the beginning of his 1991 study he notes that there have been a number of unsuccessful attempts to establish a biological basis for sexual orientation, and he footnotes the following example: "The suprachiasmatic nucleus (SCN) of the hypothalamus has been reported to be larger in homosexual than in heterosexual men . . . There is little evidence, however, to suggest that SCN is involved in regulation of sexual behavior aside from its circadian rhythmicity" (1036).

It seems to me, however, that sexuality cannot be partitioned within the hypothalamus in this way: orientation here, circadian rhythms there. The extent to which any hypothalamic function can be aside from sexuality is the very question that LeVay's study most fruitfully put into circulation. More recently, attempts have been made to study this interface between sexuality and broader hypothalamic functions. Rahman and Silber (2000) note that the SCN of the human hypothalamus is "the principal neural substrate of circadian rhythmicity" (127), and it has been found to be significantly larger in homosexual men than in heterosexual men. It follows, they argue, that sleep cycles in heterosexual and homosexual men might be different. Their data suggest that homosexual men have much shorter sleep duration than heterosexual men, the former going to sleep later and waking earlier. For a number of reasons, the data don't seem that strong (they were collected through self-report, for example). The biggest problem of the study, however, is how Rahman and Silber preserve a detached relationship among sexuality, circadian rhythms, and the hypothalamus. They remark on the correlation of sexuality and circadian rhythms and they postulate that this correlation "warrants an interpretation at the neurological level" (132), but they don't imagine the co-contamination of these events: how they might chiasmatically cross each other, constituting each other according to unusual ontologies and rhythms.

Although LeVay's data have facilitated a literature that reduces sexuality to binarized forms (Ellis and Ebertz 1997), it also opens sexuality into a broader material field. Through the LeVay study we could be provoked to think about the neurology/sexuality interface more exhaustively—not as an insular coupling, but as a node in a chiasmatic-reticulating physiological organization. It is clear enough that LeVay's 1991 report seriously simplifies sexuality and does not provide data sufficiently robust to support the conclusions that he draws there and in other contexts. It is also the case, however, that the data, generated through a conceptually awkward attempt to envisage the conjunction of neurology and sexuality, reveal a neurological complexity that LeVay has been able to record but not fully elucidate.

· · · · · · · ·   Trembling, Blushing: Darwin's Nervous System

· · · · · · · ·   Imagine a decapitated frog. This frog has lost cerebral control of its body, yet its muscular and peripheral nervous systems function normally: appropriately stimulated, the frog's limbs will move in a manner not unlike that of an intact frog. Imagine now that a drop of acid is placed on the thigh of this decapitated frog. The acid irritates the skin. The headless frog responds to this stimulant in an uncanny manner; employing a behavior that is routine for a normally functioning frog, it uses the foot on the affected leg to wipe the acid away. Imagine finally that this foot is amputated. The decapitated frog struggles for some time to remove the acid in the same manner (i.e., with its footless leg). Eventually, after reflecting on the fruitlessness of this method, the frog uses the foot on its other leg to successfully rid itself of the aggravating acid.

Early in *The Expression of the Emotions in Man and Animals*, Darwin (1872) recounts this experiment (originally performed by the German physiologist Edward Pflüger) to illuminate the complex nature of reflex actions. The frog's behavior seems to agitate against the conventional understanding of reflex action: "Reflex actions, in the strict sense of the term, are due to the excitement of a peripheral nerve, which transmits its influence to certain nerve-cells, and these in their turn excite certain muscles or glands into action; and all this may take place without any sensation or consciousness on our part" (35). The removal of head and brain eliminates consciousness or the will from the experimental scene: the decapitated frog "cannot of course feel, cannot consciously perform, any movement" (36). Even today, the reflex is defined by the absence of consciousness or intentionality, and reflexive action remains synonymous with the restricted behavioral repertoire of the lower (invertebrate) animals. The *Dictionary of Modern Biology* (Rudin 1997) defines the reflex thus: "An immediate and involuntary reaction to a stimulus without conscious initiation or modification. It is the only type of reaction in the simplest animals (for example, cnidarians) but represents only a few responses, such as the knee-jerk reaction, in animals with more sophisticated nervous systems . . . [Reflex action] is extremely rapid, as the nerve impulses bypass any processing or integration in the brain" (317).

For experimental physiologists, a decollated frog has been an excellent model for illustrating reflexive nervous action (Clarke and Jacyna 1987). A reflex is often considered to be a degraded, nonpsychological form of behavior, but the frog's behavior demonstrates otherwise. The truncation of the frog to its reflexive and peripheral substrate reveals anything but rudimentary or mindless action. The frog's peripheral nervous system demonstrates an unexpected intricacy; most pointedly, it seems to have the capacity to respond inventively. Even in this reduced, decerebrated state, the frog's nervous system is thoughtful. Its reflexivity is not circumscribed by physiological automaticity; it also embraces the antiquated denotations of reflection, consideration, return, rebound, indirect action, indirect reference, a glance or side look.[1] This simple neurophysiological action holds within it a rich behavioral and psychic world.

This scene of amphibian decapitation and reflexive action is all the more curious because Darwin uses it to advance a theory of emotional expression. In *The Expression of the Emotions in Man and Animals*, Darwin (1872) gives an account of the involuntary emotional expressions of humans in terms of the reflexive behavior of other animals: "With mankind some expressions, such as the bristling of the hair under the influence of extreme terror, or the uncovering of the teeth under that of furious rage, can hardly be understood, except on the belief that man once existed in a much lower and animal-like condition. The community of certain expressions in distinct though allied species, as in the movements of the same facial muscles during laughter by man and by various monkeys, is rendered somewhat more intelligible, if we believe their descent from a common progenitor" (12).

Darwin mobilizes the frog's nervous habits in this context to dispute the conventional detachment of human capacities from animalistic behaviors, or, to put this another way, to dispute the detachment of emotive capacities from reflexive behavior. Against Darwin, feminist and psychoanalytic commentators have tended to make a separation between human behaviors and animalistic biologies. The distinction that is made between instincts (biological, animal) and drives (linguistic, human) in Lacanian-influenced psychoanalytic criticism is one prevalent example of this division.[2] It is this critical tendency to conventionalize the character of animal biology (rudimentary!) and human behavior (complex!) that this chapter endeavors to reroute.

Darwin's concern with the reduced materialities of the nervous system in his account of the expression of emotions follows naturally from his interest in the physiology of lower animals. Prior to his voyage on the *Beagle*, and before his well-known predilection for beetle collecting was established at Cambridge, Darwin had a formative interest in aquatic invertebrates. His later published works also demonstrate a partiality for the less elevated phyla: corals, barnacles, worms.[3] Moreover, Darwin had a preference for discussion of the peripheral nervous system at the expense of elucidating higher cerebral functions. This preference seems to have been established less by any limits in his knowledge of neurology than by his early conversion to materialism, which displaced consciousness (and so its cerebral seat) from the center of evolutionary explanation. Darwin's early notebooks (1836–1844; Darwin 1987) on emotional expression locate his curiosity in the nervous body, rather than in the conscious mind-brain.

This chapter examines the generative effects of Darwin's interest in what appear to be psychologically and physiologically rudimentary events. But first I am required to take a detour through a discussion of Darwin's Lamarckism. This discussion details the relationship that Darwin established between biology and psychology, and so lays down the framework for the analysis of sympathy and blushing that closes out the chapter.

Lamarckism

My preoccupation with Darwin's preference for reductive explanations of emotional expression is further animated by his methodological reliance on one of the biological sciences' most disreputable explanatory systems: Lamarckism. Although it is Darwinism that is most often credited with bringing Lamarckism into disrepute, Darwin was as much a Lamarckian as he was a proponent of natural selection. In *The Expression of the Emotions in Man and Animals* he relies more on Lamarckian ideas than on his own theories of natural selection.

There are many reasons why the Lamarckism of *The Expression of the Emotions in Man and Animals* should not be seen as a lapse of theoretical acumen on Darwin's behalf. In the first instance, the book is enmeshed in the public articulation of Darwin's theory of natural selection. When the book was released, Darwin's theory of natural selection had reached a publication zenith: 1872 marks the sixth and final edition of *The Origin of Species*, and *The Descent of Man* had been published the previous year. Indeed, *The Expression of the Emotions in Man and Animals* covers material that Darwin had originally intended to be in *The Descent of Man*; Desmond and Moore refer to it as the "amputated head of the *Descent*" (1991, 593). Moreover, Darwin's Lamarckism is not a subordinate or accidental methodology in *The Expression of the Emotions in Man and Animals*. His notebooks and early correspondence demonstrate his many and consistent attacks on certain aspects of Lamarck's work; in particular, he rejected Lamarck's postulation that all living organisms have an innate tendency to evolve into higher forms (progressionism). Nonetheless, Darwin considered other aspects of Lamarckian evolution to be imperative to his own theoretical models.

It is argued in conventional neo-Darwinian commentaries that this reliance on Lamarckism was pressed on Darwin because modern Mendelian genetics had not yet been formulated. After Mendel, it is claimed, Darwin's Lamarckism becomes obsolete. My interests lie, not in asserting Lamarckism against modern genetics,[4] but in excavating the ways certain conceptual implications of Darwin's Lamarckism—specifically the question of the constitutive permeability of biology—remain pertinent to contemporary critical analyses of the nerves. For all these reasons, a sustained account of *The Expression of the Emotions in Man and Animals* demands an inquisitive examination of Darwin's use of Lamarckism.

Jean Baptiste Lamarck's contributions to biology were empirical, philosophical, nomenclative, and taxonomic. They included coining the term "biology" and the construction of an extensive classificatory schema of invertebrate zoology. Lamarck was an expert botanist, and as professor of zoology, insects, worms, and microscopic animals at the Musée d'Histoire Naturelle in Paris, he published a seven-volume work on the natural history of the invertebrates (Elliot 1914). However, it was Lamarck's passionate advocacy of a certain mode of evolution, specifically the thesis concerning the inheritance of acquired characteristics, that cemented his reputation not as an accomplished scientist, but as the eponymous biologist of error: "It is Lamarck's misfortune that, at least in the English-speaking world, his name has become a label for an error" (Dawkins 1986, 289).

The evolutionary mechanism to which Lamarck's name has become fixed specifies that the bodily modifications developed by organisms during their life are inherited by their offspring: "All the acquisitions or losses wrought by nature on individuals . . . are preserved by reproduction to the new individuals which arise" (Lamarck 1809, 113). Most memorably, he hypothesized that the giraffe's forelegs and neck are lengthened by the constant effort to reach leaves high up in trees. The maintenance of such efforts over time effected morphological changes (long necks, heightened forelegs) that were passed on to subsequent generations. So too, Lamarck suggested that the forelegs of the kangaroo have phylogenetically atrophied due to lack of use, swan's legs have remained short as "they make no effort to lengthen [them]" (120), and gazelles are slender and light of foot because they have "exert[ed] themselves in swift running" (122).[5]

For contemporary biology, the doctrine of the inheritance of acquired characteristics is incontrovertibly in error: "All of these processes are now rejected as incompatible with the central dogma of molecular biology, which forbids the transferral of information from the somatic tissue to the DNA of the reproductive cells" (Bowler 1992, 188). The prohibition against communication from the soma to the germline often goes under the name of Weismann's barrier. In a series of experiments in the late nineteenth century, August Weismann refuted the Lamarckism contained in Darwin's theory of pangenesis by demonstrating that the constituents of reproductive cells are not affected by changes in the rest of the body. Irrespective of somatic modification, the contents of reproductive cells are passed on unchanged from one generation to the next. Inheritance—now under the sole proprietorship of the germline—was rigorously demarcated from somatic development: "The popularity of Lamarckism arose largely from the fact that it was a natural extension of a pregenetical way of looking at reproduction, in which growth and inheritance were seen as aspects of a single integrated phenomenon. The separation of growth and development from transmission by modern genetics has robbed Lamarckism of its basic plausibility" (Bowler 1992, 188).

The antagonism of Lamarckism and Darwinism has been one of the means by which contemporary biological plausibility and implausibility are discriminated. These days, Darwin's tenacious preference for the inheritance of acquired characteristics is ignored or undertheorized, and the censure of Lamarck's "notorious heresy" (Dennett 1995, 321) has become increasingly strict. The direction and effects of such censure are nowhere more articulately expressed than in Daniel Dennett's brief rejection of the inheritance of acquired characteristics in his spirited defense of Darwinism. A footnote at the beginning of this critique elucidates the wider theoretical context within which Lamarck's implausibility is to be located: "I restrict Lamarckism to inheritance of acquired characteristics *through the genetic apparatus*. If we relax the definition, then Lamarckism is not clearly a fallacy. After all, human beings inherit (by legacy) acquired wealth from their parents, and most animals inherit (by proximity) acquired parasites from their parents, and some animals inherit (by succession) acquired nests, burrows, dens from their parents. These are all phenomena of biological significance, but they are not what Lamarck was getting at—heretically" (321).

That is, the inheritance of acquired characteristics only makes sense as an error when it is mobilized to give an account of biological systems. In nonbiological spheres, the heresy of Lamarckism is transformed into the good sense of basic psychological, sociological, and economic theory. It is clear enough (to Dennett, at least) that money, privilege, bad habits, emotional trauma, cultural etiquette, and ethical norms can be developed and then transmitted from parent to child and from one cultural sphere to another. Although these modes of inheritance may find themselves interrupted or inhibited, in principle they are not confined—as a biological system is—to the narrow corridor of molecular modes of transmission.

This division between biological and nonbiological modes of inheritance is widely accepted. Psychoanalysis, for example, has explained how psychic inheritance is subject to peculiar spatial and chronological mechanisms of transmission (condensation, displacement, deferred action). Once psychic trauma has been sparked in an individual, it may be disseminated across other bodies and, sadly, across many generations; often, it is transformed into different material configurations (cultural trauma, mediatized affect, somatic symptomology), reverberating back onto the individual in ways that modify (intensify, attenuate, inhibit) the very nature of the traumatizing event. In a Freudian schema, inheritance could be called Lamarckian—quite uncontroversially: the psychic modifications undergone by individuals due to the vicissitude of their environment are often passed on to offspring, peers, and bystanders. Drawing on psychoanalytic theory, many contemporary critical psychologies, sociologies, anthropologies, and histories have described the complex and expansive nature of such psychocultural transferences. Yet none of these mechanisms is attributed to biological domains.

Ona Nierenberg (1998), for example, attempts to negotiate between the folly of Freud's acceptance of biological Lamarckism and the critical usefulness of phylogenetic fantasy that this Lamarckism spawned: "Freud's phylogenetic fantasies have been expelled from psychoanalytic theory on the ground of their scientific and anthropological inaccuracy . . . In fact, the Lamarckian idea of the inheritance of acquired characteristics was already widely discredited by the time Freud expressed an interest in it . . . and Freud held fast to this interest up until the very end of his work, by which time it had certainly been expelled from the domain of legitimate science" (234–235). For Nierenberg, "the concept of phylogenetic fantasies does not stand or fall with the scientific status of Lamarckian theory" (235). As with so much contemporary critical Freudian commentary, Nierenberg's analysis relies on her ability to disavow the biologism of Freud's work. The manner in which the biology of Freud's Lamarckism is accepted as naïvely erroneous, yet the psychological aspects of that Lamarckism are cogently deployed (Nierenberg's defense of phylogenetic fantasies is eloquent and authoritative) is the issue I am addressing here. This too easy division (a kind of ontological apartheid) implies that the stuff of biology and the stuff of psychology operate in disjunctive realms. In particular, biological inheritance has been stripped of the infectious, communicative, expansive characteristics that are routinely attributed to psychocultural systems.

Despite the wide philosophical and political differences that must separate them, Nierenberg and Dennett agree that mechanisms of inheritance that are expansively communicative are psychologically plausible yet biologically fallacious. Dennett's insistence that Lamarckian inheritance is credible in every material system except a biological one generates a grander form of Weismann's barrier. "Dennett's barrier" decrees that the mechanisms of transmission and inheritance that are natural to the psychological, social, economic, and cultural spheres (so natural, so self-evident, so straightforward that their explication can be contained to a footnote) are not operative in the realm of biology. Behind Dennett's barrier, biological matter—now Weismann's germline writ large—is impervious to the somatic modifications of psychology and culture.

It is the argument of this chapter that the impermeability of the biological realm to a wide range of mechanisms of inheritance, transmission, and transformation is a decidedly un-Darwinian presumption. Darwin's system of evolution specifies the ontological coimplication of animals, man, plants, rocks, and emotions. Each mode of materiality is built through its complicitous relations to the others, and heredity is governed by a heterogeneous set of forces. In an enthusiastic preface to the 1965 edition of *The Expression of the Emotions in Man and Animals,* Konrad Lorenz reaffirms what he sees as a central lesson in Charles Darwin's text: that "behavior patterns have an evolution exactly like that of organs" (xii). Psychology and biology are so thoroughly homologous, Lorenz claims, that behavioral patterns could be as reliable a measure of species differentiation as "the forms of bones, teeth, or any other bodily structures" (xii). This is no small claim on Lorenz's part. An explanation of how species differentiate (the origin of species) is at the core of Darwin's theory of evolution. By claiming that behavior patterns could be used to distinguish among species as reliably as organic structures, Lorenz folds psychology into the heart of evolutionary explanation. By accentuating the structural intimacy of biology and psychology in *The Expression of the Emotions in Man and Animals*, Lorenz hints at one of the most underexamined aspects of Darwin's work: that evolution is not narrowly or primarily a biological process. Every one of Darwin's texts attests that the stuff of evolution is radically heterogeneous; certainly it is biological, but it is also psychological, cultural, geological, oceanic, and meteorological. We have been encouraged to think of the relations among these evolutionary forces as somewhat unilateral (the effects of the geological on the cultural; the effects of the biological on the psychological), yet a closer examination of Darwin's work reveals a reciprocally configured system.

Positioning himself against Lamarck's heretical notions, Dennett argues for the radicality of Darwin's thesis of natural selection: "It is not just a wonderful scientific idea. It is a dangerous idea" (1995, 21). However, in these neo-Darwinian times the real wonder and danger of Darwin's system lie in his cultivation of a permeable, heterogeneously constituted biology. The substantive barriers that Weismann and Dennett have so vigilantly protected are profoundly antievolutionary. By disconnecting biology from its constitutive relations with other ontological systems, biology becomes isolated and destitute. The barriers behind which biology has been sequestered do not annul the secondary relations that biology has on other systems (e.g., the effects of neurotransmitter uptake on psychological mood), and it is these kinds of causal relations that neo-Darwinian commentaries seek to exploit. These barriers do, however, obstruct the operations of a more originary relational network (worm-man-timidity-chalk-buildings-vegetation-rain) within which biology is constituted, animated, and evolved.[6]

Sympathy

Perhaps the most routine and widely circulated account of *The Expression of Emotions in Man and Animals* is that it advocates a relation of phylogenetic determinism between biology and human emotions: humans emote as they do because they have inherited older biological structures and functions that dictate the bodily and psychological parameters of anger, joy, sadness, and shame. In these accounts, human emotions are either vestiges of primitive behavioral responses or the adaptive outcome of millions of years of natural selection on hominid form and function. It is not my intent to argue, in an agonistic fashion, that human emotions are disconnected from phylogenetic and biological constraints, that they are uniquely human or culture-bound faculties. On the contrary, I take Darwin's conjunction of psychology and biology very seriously, but I want to turn the scholarly and political implications of this interface in directions other than that usually taken by his high-profile commentators (Dawkins, Dennett, E. O. Wilson).

At the beginning of *The Expression of the Emotions in Man and Animals* Darwin offers three principles that account for the involuntarily emotional expressions and gestures used by man and other animals:[7]

1. The principle of serviceable associated habits, which describes the manner by which certain expressions or postures that were once volitional have become reflexive and inheritable forms of emotional expression. For example, the aggressive posture of dogs (lowered head, crouching), which "has become hereditary in our pointers and setters" (Darwin 1872, 43), was originally the habit of carnivorous animals as they approached prey.

2. The principle of antithesis, which describes how opposing emotional states are expressed through antithetical physical gestures: opposite frames

of mind are accompanied by opposite bodily actions. For example, the angry cat has an open mouth, flat ears, and bristled fur; the affectionate cat has a closed mouth, erect ears, and flat fur. These opposite actions are involuntary and are explicable only as expressions of the complete opposite or antithesis of a more primary attitude.

3. The principle of direct action of the nervous system, which describes how certain emotional expressions are the direct effect of the constitution of the nervous system (trembling, blushing, perspiring, fainting).

This third principle governing the nervous system appears to be the most constrictive of these three maxims: "Certain actions, which we recognise as expressive of certain states of mind, are the direct result of the constitution of the nervous system, and have been from the first independent of the will, and, to a large extent, of habit" (66). This principle states that some emotive responses are simply native to the nervous system. The nervous actions associated with these emotional expressions function independently of the will and are little affected by the vicissitudes of habit. Darwin offers some examples of this direct action of the nervous system: the secretion of tears, the erection of body hair, the incontinence of certain organs or glands, the racing of the heart. Trembling is perhaps exemplary of the direct action of the nervous system. Independent of the will, trembling is a behavioral response that these days we would say is hardwired into the nervous system. No routine of habit, no effort of self-control will be able to override the reflexive impetus of the nervous system once activated by a strong emotion like terror or joy.

However, the extent to which Darwin is able to keep nervous action separate from the psychological realm (volition and habit) has already been undermined by his first principle. There Darwin argues, via Lamarckian mechanisms, that certain behaviors and gestures that are now used reflexively to express emotions were originally (i.e., in the phylogenetic past) performed voluntarily: "Some actions, which were at first performed consciously, have become through habit and association converted into reflex actions, and are now so firmly fixed and inherited, that they are performed, even when not of the least use" (39–40). Indeed, he explains the reflexive behavior of the decapitated frog in this way: "It is scarcely credible that the movements of a headless frog, when it wipes off a drop of acid or other object from its thigh, and which movements are so well co-ordinated for a special purpose, were not at first performed voluntarily, being afterwards rendered easy through long-continued habit so as at last to be performed unconsciously, or independently, of the cerebral hemispheres" (40).

The frog experiment demonstrates how ontogenetic habits have passed into phylogenetic reflexes—how the habitual repetition of specific gestures over many generations has rendered them reflexive and inheritable across the whole species. So effective and so widespread is this phylogenetic inheritance of emotional expression, Darwin claims, that these acquired expressions can hardly be distinguished from direct nervous action.

Throughout *The Expression of the Emotions in Man and Animals* Darwin attempts to hold separate the expressive mechanisms described by the principle of habitual acquisition and those described by the principle of nervous action, yet the anecdotes and empirical fragments that constitute the text's main argument persistently thwart this maneuver. As Darwin admits, "A brief consideration of the outward signs of some of the stronger sensations and emotions will best serve to show us . . . in how complex a manner the principle . . . of the direct action of the excited nervous system of the body, is combined with the principle of habitually associated, serviceable movements" (69).

Darwin's domestic experiment with one of his children demonstrates the complex manner in which direct nervous action (neurophysiology) is complicit with acquired habits (psychology). Darwin shakes an empty box close to the face of his infant child when it is 114 days old. The child does not reflexively blink. However, when something is put in the box to make a rattling sound, and it is again shaken in front of the child, the child "blinked its eyes violently every time and started a little" (39). Darwin's explanation of these experimental results weaves together ontogenetic learning, Lamarckian inheritance, and direct nervous action: "It was obviously impossible that a carefully-guarded infant could have learnt by experience that a rattling sound near it eyes indicated danger to them. But such experience will have been slowly gained at a later age during a long series of generations; and from what we know of inheritance, there is nothing improbable in the transmission of a habit to the offspring at an earlier age than that at which it was first acquired by the parents" (39).

Firmly fixed reflexive actions like the eyeblink differ from more malleable predispositions, not in their biology or character, but in the chronology of their acquisition: "There has been more than enough [time] for these habits to have become innate or converted into reflex actions; for they are common to most or all of the common quadrupeds, and must therefore have been first acquired at a very remote period" (40). For Darwin, a hardwired reflex is simply a habit of great phylogenetic age.

If the startle/eyeblink reflex could be routed through phylogenetic habit (it was "originally acquired by the habit of jumping away as quickly as possible from danger," 40), then is every action of the nervous system also constituted through the principle of Lamarckian acquisition? Is any nervous action direct, or do they all have an originary complicity with habitual repetition, volition, or cogitation? Regressing back further and further phylogenetically, Darwin negates his third principle by describing most nervous reflexes as acquired habits. It is the contraction of the iris muscle in the eye that eventually gives content to the rapidly shrinking category of direct nervous action, and so halts the spread of Lamarckian explanation. Darwin claims that the contraction of the iris "cannot possibly have been at first voluntarily performed and then fixed by habit; for the iris is not known to be under the conscious control of the will in any animal" (41). Unadulterated by consciousness or the will, the contraction of the iris is an action guided solely and directly by the nervous system. With this breakdown of Lamarckian justification, "some explanation, quite distinct from habit, will have to be discovered" (41). In a rare moment in the text, Darwin turns to the explanatory power of natural selection: if radiating nerve force causes the iris muscle to contract and thus advantageously protects the eye from too much illumination, then this mechanism "might afterwards have been taken advantage of and modified for special purposes" (41).

Darwin's iris example appears to erect a barrier past which Lamarckian influence cannot extend. The motor pathways of the nervous system are thus divided into different modalities: nervous substrate that is allied with consciousness and volition, and nervous substrate that is detached from such psychological influence. In contemporary terms, this is the distinction between the somatic (or voluntary) nervous system (which governs the skeletal muscles that are under conscious control) and the autonomic nervous system (which controls the smooth muscles, cardiac muscles, and glands of the body via the sympathetic, parasympathetic, and enteric systems). On closer inspection, however, both Darwin and contemporary neurophysiological nomenclature attest to the ways direct (automatic) nervous action is implicated from the beginning in indirect, reflective systems. The use of the term sympathetic in relation to the nervous system dates back to Galen: " 'Sympathy,' or its Latin equivalent 'consensus,' was a rapport thought to exist between parts of the body, especially the organs, that were not anatomically connected . . . As Galen had originally pointed out, this involuntary interrelationship of sympathetic harmony in the body was effected by way of nerves or blood vessels" (Clarke and Jacyna 1987, 102).

Sympathy was usually deployed clinically to explain strange affinities in disease states (e.g., the kinship of nasal symptoms with uterine diseases). Distant organs were thought to respond sympathetically to another organ's anguish, thus generating puzzling organic alliances. The sympathetic nature of these symptoms was later revealed to be due to reflex actions; "the term 'sympathetic response' remained in use and synonymous with 'reflex' until the nineteenth century" (Clarke and Jacyna 1987, 104). So, rather than liberating biology from this eccentric notion of interorgan alliances, modern physiology has condensed sympathy into the structure and function of the autonomic nervous system. The vestigial terminology of "sympathetic" and "parasympathetic" registers the long established character of nervous substrate: a reflexive affinity for other organs and bodies.

Darwin's own nervous system painfully confirmed this kinship of neurophysiology with other organs and bodies. For most of his adult life, Darwin was plagued by a nervous condition that was so debilitating it left him unable to work for long periods of time. This condition, clearly exacerbated by stressful psychological and emotional events, encompassed vomiting, nausea, heart palpitations, lethargy, and spots before the eyes. One of the most distressing sympathetic events to befall Darwin's nervous system was the death of his favorite daughter, Annie. At a time when his own nervous condition was in remission for the first time in years, Annie fell terminally ill with symptoms that closely mimicked her father's chronic complaint. As he watched his daughter succumb to "Bilious Fever with typhoid character," Darwin's stomach condition returned acutely, and he was confined to his sickbed as Annie died (Desmond and Moore 1991). In both Darwin and modern neurophysiology there is something sympathetic in so-called direct nervous action. Reflexive, hardwired, involuntary responses always owe a debt to earlier psychological proclivities, preferences, and habits, and beyond that to other bodies and other systems of inheritance and transmission.

Perhaps, then, the lessons to be drawn from the case of the contracting iris are not as straightforward as they might appear. Removing the iris from any phylogenetic contact with volition (i.e., renouncing Lamarckian explanation), Darwin appears to reveal a bedrock of pure nervous action. Yet the eye caused Darwin no small amount of trouble. Desmond and Moore (1991) recount an early scene of this difficulty with the eye, pointing to one of the routes by which the eye was to become an exemplary evolutionary puzzle. Early in his career, Darwin decided to show his unpublished essay on evolution (written in 1842) to his devoutly religious wife, Emma. "She sat with the pile of papers, pointing out unclear passages, leaving tell-tale notes in the margin, showing where she disagreed. 'A great assumption/E. D.' she scribbled against his claim that the human eye 'may *possibly* have been acquired by gradual selection of slight but in each case useful deviations.' He softened the passage still more; but, from then on, the piecemeal evolution of a complex, integrated organ like the eye left him in a cold sweat" (319–320).

The eye recurs in Darwin's work and in evolutionary commentaries generally in the most equivocal terms. Rather than being the example on which a theory of direct neurological action could be grounded, the eye epitomizes the unsettling nature of evolutionary itineraries. When Darwin reaches the example of the contracting iris in *The Expression of the Emotions in Man and Animals*, his explanation via natural selection is fleeting and unexpectedly flimsy. It is the strange logic of inherited habits that is more plausible; it is the principle of direct action that appears peculiar. In fact, the example of the contracting iris, read in context, renders suspicious any notion of neurophysiological action as direct, sovereign, and self-evident. The plausibility of Darwin's last-minute consolidation of non-Lamarckian direct nervous action has been undermined by the inventive notion of nervous action that he promulgates elsewhere and which he has exemplified so sensationally in the actions of the decapitated frog.

Blushing

The final chapter of *The Expression of the Emotions in Man and Animals* is devoted to one of human biology's most curious inventions: blushing. After presenting anthropological evidence for the universality of blushing in humans, Darwin turns his attention to its causes. He notes that blushing is the engorgement of the facial capillaries with blood. In contemporary neurophysiological terms, blushing is under the governance of the autonomic nervous system; the smooth muscles encircling the facial capillaries are relaxed under the influence of the sympathetic nervous system, allowing greater blood flow to the face (Curtis and Barnes 1989, 759–760).

At first glance, blushing appears to be a straightforward physiological event. Similar, perhaps, to the involuntary nature of trembling. As I argued above, however, these so-called direct nervous actions are always more complexly configured; so it is with blushing. Darwin's argument about the causes of blushing is twofold: first, "we cannot cause a blush . . . by any physical means—that is by any other action of the body. It is the mind which must be affected" (1872, 309–310). Whereas laughter can be brought upon us by tickling the skin, fear by the threat of bodily harm, and anger by the delivery of such a blow, blushing cannot be directly induced by a bodily event. What causes the capillaries to enlarge and thus redden the face with blood is not "any physical means" but rather a psychological action. The etiology of blushing must be mapped through the mind. The second part of Darwin's argument follows quickly from this. In truth, it is not my mind that causes the capillaries of my face to be swollen with blood, it is what is in the mind of another person that has this influence: "It is not the simple act of reflecting on our appearance, but the thinking of what others think of us, which excites a blush" (325). Blushing is an intersubjective event. In particular, Darwin argues, it is the attention of others on us (especially on the face and the exposed parts of the body) that causes us to blush. A medical report of an institutionalized woman illustrates the flushing effect of attention on the body:

> On the morning after [the patient's] arrival in the Asylum, Dr. Browne, together with his assistants, visited her whilst she was in bed. The

moment that he approached, she blushed deeply over her cheeks and temples; and the blush spread quickly to her ears. She was much agitated and tremulous. He unfastened the collar of her chemise in order to examine the state of her lungs; and then a brilliant blush rushed over her chest, in an arched line over the upper third of each breast, and extended downwards between the breasts nearly to the ensiform cartilage of the sternum. This case is interesting, as the blush did not thus extend downwards until it became intense by her attention being drawn to this part of her person. (313)

Blushing is an event in which the very nature of muscles, nerves, and blood cannot be separated from the thoughts and actions of another. As such, it illustrates one aspect of the entangled nature of the biology-psychology interface particularly well: biology does not act without psychology. Even events governed by reflexive (autonomic) systems are embroiled in and amplified by psychic action. If the phenomenology of blushing is familiar enough, the neurophysiological mechanisms at play are less easily named. Because conventional neurophysiological explanations are formulated as though the nervous system is autonomously constituted, there is no ready manner for explaining neurophysiologically how nerves, blood vessels, and muscles can be so acutely attuned to, and held captive by, the thoughts and actions of others. What is the anatomy, physiology, and biochemistry of the capillaries of this patient's face, neck, ears, breasts, and sternum such that they can be so agonizingly sensitive to the doctor, his assistants, and their observational routines? It has been my argument in the previous sections that Darwin's use of Lamarck helps to form a frame of reference for these uncanny psychosomatic events. By keeping biology in contact with the vicissitudes of other material systems (psychic, cultural, geological) Darwin's work allows an expansive understanding of the nature of neurophysiological events to emerge.

Even the inheritance of blushing can be opened up to a wider set of influences. Again, an anecdote is Darwin's most insightful commentary:

The tendency to blush is inherited. Dr. Burgess gives the case of a family consisting of a father, mother, and ten children, all of whom, without exception, were prone to blush to a most painful degree. The children were grown up; "and some of them were sent to travel in order to wear away this diseased sensibility, but nothing was of the slightest avail." Even peculiarities of blushing seem to be inherited. Sir James Paget, whilst examining the spine of a girl, was struck at her singular manner of blushing; a big splash of red appeared first on one cheek, and then other splashes, various scattered over the face and neck. He subsequently asked the mother whether her daughter always blushed in this peculiar manner; and was answered "Yes, she takes after me." Sir J. Paget then perceived that by asking this question he had caused the mother to blush; and she exhibited the same peculiarity as her daughter. (311)

This anecdote suggests that the inheritance of blushing is more than a narrow molecular transaction. It is also more than a socially constructed routine. The physiological sympathy among mother, daughter, and doctor transverses conventional distinctions between inheritance and development, volition and reflex, hardwired and cultured actions. To say that such action is biologically inherited tells only part of the story. Without question, this incident is indebted to genetic legacy in the standard scientific sense. Without question, this event is also indebted to Victorian sensibility. A more resonant kind of explanation of this event, however, needs to be able to say how these two domains (the biogenetic and the psychocultural) are materially intertwined. What both of Darwin's blushing anecdotes hint at is that the curious rendering psychological of neurophysiological action is not a secondary accident to which biological matter may or may not fall victim. It is not a contingent or happenstance event. Rather, psychocultural tendencies are at play in the microstructure of all neurophysiological events—even the most reflexive.

Darwin claims that blushing is an emotional response that is unique to humans. The amphibian face does not burn with acute self-consciousness. The amphibian nervous system does, however, display a peripheral inventiveness that is closely allied with the nervous mechanisms of blushing. Both the frog and the mother express the complex psychophysiology of biological matter; both show that direct nervous action is always in intimate sympathy with other organs, other bodies, and other systems. If there is precious little in the way of a theory of emotion to be found in *The Expression of the Emotions in Man and Animals*, the reader is nonetheless compensated with a model of nervous action that brings a frog's limbs and a mother's face into a generative, sympathetic, and psychological alliance. This alliance of mother and frog, emotion and neurophysiology is one of the most useful contributions made in *The Expression of the Emotions in Man and Animals*, and it attests to the usefulness of Darwin's work for thinking neurology critically.

· · · · · · · ·   5

· · · · · · · ·   Emotional Lizards: Evolution

and the Reptilian Brain

· · · · · · · ·   A man is sitting on his front porch. Oliver Sacks has
come to visit him. Sacks is in Guam to investigate a neurological disorder
that is endemic to the island. The *lytico-bodig* is a disease that manifests in
two forms: lytico is a progressive paralysis that is similar to motor neuron
disease; bodig is a parkinsonian-like condition. The man that Sacks has
come to visit has become "almost petrified with the bodig" (Sacks 1996, 177).
Like so many similarly affected individuals on Guam, this man is motionless
and has developed a fixed stare.

One of the central concerns of Sacks's narratives has been to show that
neurological disorder is marked by more than loss or deficit or disruption.
Often, neurological conditions reveal a psychological or behavioral capacity
that has been obstructed by normal neurological functioning; for example,
the loss of color vision generates grief and confusion but also renewed
artistic productivity; the arrest of human affectivity that cuts a woman off
from emotional contact with other people generates an intense sympathy for
animals (Sacks 1995). On the porch in Guam, then, Sacks sees more than loss
of spontaneous movement; he sees in this man a mode of existence that has
become differently ordered. For Sacks, this man's fixed gaze is not "a blank
staring, a staring at nothing, but an almost painfully engrossed, wistful
staring . . . [The man sits] on his porch, unblinking, unmoving, motionless
as a tortoise . . . an enraptured spectator" (1996, 177).

The evolutionary antecedents of this man's newly emerged reptilian manner are explored by Sacks in an extended footnote: "It is sometimes said (the
term goes back to Charcot) that patients with Parkinson's disease have a
'reptilian' stare. This is not just a picturesque (or pejorative) metaphor;

normal access to the motor functions, which gives mammals their delicate motor flexibility, is impaired in parkinsonism; this leads to alternations of extreme immobility with sudden, almost explosive motion, which are reminiscent of some reptiles" (Sacks 1996, 281).

Characteristically, Sacks is less interested in the deficits that the bodig produces than in the reptilian manner it uncovers. His primary concern is not how impairment of motor functions curtails mammalian function, but how neurological disease replaces one kind of motor regime with another: explosive reptilian motion where previously there had been delicate motor flexibility. As the footnote continues, Sacks elaborates on this relation between reptilian and mammalian functions; perhaps reptilian character in humans is the return of what has been phylogenetically repressed: "Parkinson himself was a palaeontologist, as well as a physician, and his 1804 book, *Organic Remains of a Former World*, is one of the great pioneer texts of palaeontology. One wonders whether he may have partly regarded parkinsonism as an atavism, a reversion, the uncovering, through disease, of an ancestral, 'an antediluvian' mode of function dating from the ancient past" (281–282).

One might have expected that Sacks would turn to Freud's figuration of the unconscious as a buried archaeological stratum to explain antediluvian modes of function in humans.[1] Instead, he reverts to earlier authors, first Charcot and then Parkinson, and to earlier epochs to depict human neurobiology as a paleontological formation. For Sacks, the human brain cannot be circumscribed by what has accrued culturally (archaeologically); it is also the product of what has accrued biologically (paleontologically). That is, what has evolved as human brain tissue is not only the consequence of millennia of hominid experience, but also the effect of vast periods of vertebrate development: fish brains, primate brains, reptile brains, bird brains.

Reptilian Character

In Darwinian and neo-Darwinian models of evolution, reptilian characteristics in humans are vestiges of past commonalities. What is reptilian in humans is a remnant of previous, now extinct bodily form (e.g., the stem reptiles, from which modern reptiles, birds, placentals, and mammals evolved; see figure 3). Sacks's ruminations are consonant with the established notion of evolution as a branching system. Rather than formulating evolution as a ladder of progress in which organisms evolve in a direct and linear fashion out of each other (first fish, then reptiles, then birds), contemporary evolutionary theories depict the emergence of new forms as a branching development: from a common root all manner of different spe-

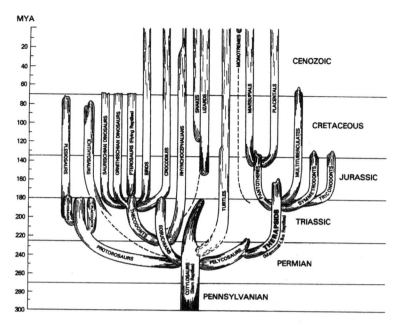

Figure 3. Phylogeny of reptiles. Reprinted with permission from MacLean 1990, 34.

cies diverge. Reptiles and mammals, for example, evolved along quite different lines once divergence from the stem reptiles in the Permian period occurred some 230 million years ago. Having now branched away from each other, current-day reptiles and mammals have no mutual influence; their evolutionary relations are in the past and their bodily connections are vestigial.[2]

I want to highlight in Sacks a less conventional map of evolutionary influence. Without dismissing the branches of lineage laid down in conventional models, Sacks also keeps the bodily connection between long-separated lines active. That is, his reptilian-mammalian patient embodies evolutionary relations not simply along branch lines (stem reptiles–mammal-like reptiles–placentals), but also across already differentiated lines in the present (reptiles-mammals). This latter kind of relation, a bodily connection that traverses the branching system, makes evolution a networked array in which bodily form isn't just influenced by the past, but is also generated by a biological commerce between classes and species in the present.[3] As he finishes his footnote about his bodig patient, Sacks remarks on another transversion in human neurobiology:

> Whether or not this [atavistic tendency] is so of parkinsonism is arguable, but one can certainly see reversion to, or disclosure of, a variety of

primitive behaviours in post-encephalitic syndromes on occasion, and in a rare condition, branchial myoclonus,[4] arising from lesions of the brain stem. Here there occur rhythmic movements in the palate, middle-ear muscles, and certain muscles in the neck—an odd and unintelligible pattern, until one realizes that these are the only vestiges of the gill arches, the branchial musculature, in man. Branchial myoclonus is, in effect, a gill movement in man, a revelation of the fact that we carry our fishy ancestors, our evolutionary precursors, within us. (1996, 281–282)

The reptilian manner of Sacks's bodig patient demonstrates that one of the most important divisions of the vertebrate line (cold-blooded and warm-blooded) remains extant and active within the highly specialized structures of human neurobiology: fish, reptile, mammal are neurobiologically coeval. As phyla and classes and species have differentiated they have retained the traces of their ancestral forms, keeping for each individual the capacity to resemble not just its parents, but also its cousin species and classes (the other progeny of the stem reptiles). Sacks's associations (reptiles-mammals-paleontology-human-brainstem-gills) emphasize propinquity between distantly related species, irrespective of direct lines of descent; this intimate, miscegenating array of connections among organisms is an exemplary Darwinian formulation (as I explain shortly). With the example of branchial myoclonus Sacks hints that evolutionary effects don't just emerge from the past, they also traverse the now established branches of differentiated classes and species.

For Sacks, the emergence of reptilian mannerisms in his patient is not a degeneration to subhuman form. Such a figuration of the bodig would presume that the human is primarily and perhaps purely mammalian. Instead, Sacks is interested in how the human is produced by the consanguinity of mammalian, reptilian, and fishlike characteristics in the present. He considers atavism to be the uncovering of a current connection, not just an uncovering of an ancient link. If we still carry our fishy ancestors within us, it is not simply as vestigial freight—as inert, dead weight to which we are reduced in pathological or traumatic circumstances. If there are vestigial gills in our necks, this suggests a fishlike quality to human nature.

Sacks's work is powerful not simply because of its ability to resist degenerative understandings of neurological disorder, but also because it demonstrates how different modes of embodiment (reptilian, mammalian, neurological, emotional, behavioral, cultural) intermesh, cohabit, and occasionally dissociate. It is this approach that makes Sacks's work instructive for feminists interested in neurobiological embodiment. Hitherto, feminist and cultural theorists have had considerable reservations about biological theories of emotion; neurological theories have been considered too reductive, and evolutionary theories too interested in phylogenetic determinism. This chapter is concerned with elucidating the kinds of evolutionary theories that may be useful for building theories of affective embodiment that are astute in both feminist and neuroscientific terms.

The importance of building new conceptual models of the affects is being felt simultaneously in cultural studies and in the neurosciences. And despite the considerable methodological differences between these domains, each has become interested in affect theories that draw on evolutionary tenets. In relation to cultural studies, I am thinking of the burgeoning interest in Silvan Tomkins's (1962–1991) theory of affect, which revivifies a Darwinian model of emotion; likewise, evolutionary theories have been central to the emerging interest in the neurobiology of emotion (Damasio 1994, 1999; LeDoux 1996; Panksepp 1998). Attempts to think emotion innovatively in the humanities are beginning to exploit this confluence of neurological, evolutionary, and psychological data. Sedgwick and Frank's (1995) critique of the antibiological convictions of many humanities-based models of affect has been timely in this regard. They suggest that the ongoing viability of feminist, queer, and other critical endeavors may well depend on their ability to engage more seriously, less incredulously with scientific theories. In particular, they stress the importance of engaging with scientific theories that cut across accepted critical doctrines about biology and subjectivity. It is not just a matter of recruiting scientific data that already confirm feminist schemata, but of seeing how some scientific data can reorder and rejuvenate feminist theories of embodiment. Sacks's model of enmeshing mammalian and reptilian embodiments in his bodig patient has been my starting point for this conceptual exploration.

My argument in this chapter is that evolutionary and neurological accounts of the emotions could be immensely useful for feminist theories of affectivity and embodiment. I do not review the current state of neuroscientific research on emotion; in this sense, I do not take scientific data to be the last word on the nature of affectivity. Nonetheless, there are conceptual innovations in this scientific research (even when it is empirically outmoded) that can help feminists build more robust models of embodiment and emotion. The central focus of this chapter, then, is conceptual: using Sacks and Darwin, and the popular writings of neurologists Paul MacLean and Joseph LeDoux, this chapter explores how simplistic divisions between emotion and cognition, brain and body, animal and human can be rethought neurologically. This neurobiological research has not considered questions of gender; nonetheless, I contend that its innovative approach to the psychobiology of affect provides a useful conceptual framework for feminists interested in engaging with neuroscientific data.

Since the 1950s, neurobiologist Paul MacLean has been elaborating a model of the human brain that draws directly on evolutionary principles and that gives an important role to reptilian structures and functions. MacLean's model of the "triune brain" has been enormously influential on both empirical and theoretical research on the human brain, especially in relation to neurological theories of emotion. MacLean promoted the idea of a limbic system in the human brain that mediates emotional responses. The idea of a circumscribed emotional system in the brain is now usually disputed by neuroscientists working on emotion, but the triune brain remains an important conceptual model for a number of reasons. First, this model captured the popular and scientific imagination about emotion. It is still commonplace to see references in both popular and scientific literatures to a discrete, deeply buried emotional brain. Second, the emotional brain is often confused with the reptilian brain, even though MacLean's model makes a clear distinction between limbic (emotional) and reptilian formations. A clear elucidation of the tenets of the triune brain remains valuable. Third, although MacLean's model is often dismissed as simplistic and neurobiologically outmoded, the conceptual details of this model (how the various parts of the system fit together) are more astute than is usually supposed. In this section I lay out the framework of MacLean's model and make a case that, notwithstanding its flaws, this is a model that strives to think of evolutionary relations in the brain in useful ways.

MacLean's model divides the human forebrain[5] into three formations: reptilian, paleomammalian (the limbic system), and neomammalian (see figure 4). Each part of this triune structure can be differentiated, MacLean (1990) argues, in functional, biochemical, and anatomical terms. In the forebrain there are "three basic evolutionary formations that reflect an ancestral relationship to reptiles, early mammals, and recent mammals . . . Radically different in chemistry and structure and in an evolutionary sense countless generations apart, the three neural assemblies constitute a hierarchy of three-brains-in-one, a triune brain. Based on these features alone, it might be surmised that psychological and behavioral functions depend on the interplay of three quite different mentalities . . . [Each evolutionary formation has] its own special intelligence, its own subjectivity, its own sense of time and space, and its own memory, motor, and other functions" (8–9).

The triune structure is as follows. At the base of the forebrain is a group of ganglionic structures that MacLean names the "protoreptilian formation" or "R-complex" or "reptilian complex." Traditionally, these structures have been thought to be involved in basic bodily movement and some very rudimentary behavioral responses. On the basis of his research on lizards and

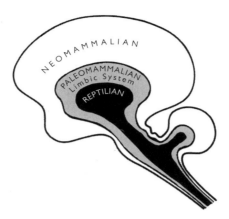

Figure 4. Symbolic representation of the triune brain.
Reprinted with permission from MacLean 1990, 9.

other reptiles, however, MacLean has given the protoreptilian formation a broader functional profile: this includes "the struggle for power, adherence to routine, 'imitation,' obeisance to precedent, and deception" (16). Sacks draws on this kind of orientation, I suspect, in his ruminations about his bodig patient. By attributing these kinds of complex responses to the reptilian complex, MacLean displaces the classical reductionist expectation that parts of the brain that are older, in evolutionary terms, govern behaviors that are rudimentary. Never say higher and lower, as Darwin scribbled in his copy of Robert Chambers's *Vestiges of the Natural History of Creation*. Sacks enters into the spirit of such formulations of reptilian behaviors when he sees in his patient a different mode of comportment ("not a blank staring, a staring at nothing, but an almost painfully engrossed, wistful staring . . . an enraptured spectator") rather than a primitive, inhuman state.

Above this reptilian formation lies the limbic system, or what MacLean calls the paleomammalian formation. MacLean argues that the limbic system brokers maternal care, audiovocal communication, and play. Reptiles, which lack a paleomammalian formation, do not exhibit maternal care, they do not play, and they are mute. This part of the human forebrain is thought to play a crucial role in the generation and regulation of emotional behavior. MacLean's model suggests that affectivity is a capacity beyond the reach of reptilian structure. It is only with the emergence of mammals that passions and sympathies come to motivate and animate behavior, a difference we recognize in the colloquial distinction between cold-blooded and warm-blooded.[6]

Highest of all in this triune structure is the neomammalian formation, which comprises the upper cortical surfaces. It is this formation that has expanded so rapidly in primate species in recent evolutionary history.

MacLean is keen to point out that the triune brain is not a conventional evolutionary structure: "It is perhaps worth noting . . . that some workers misinterpret the triune concept as implying a consecutive layering of the three main neural assemblies, somewhat analogous to strata of rock" (1990, 9). The prominent Cambridge neuroscientist Susan Greenfield (2000), for example, summarizes the functional aspects of the triune model in precisely these terms: "MacLean had the novel insight that not only was the brain stem held in check by the limbic system, but that the limbic system in turn was suppressed by the cortex" (5). Greenfield sees in the triune model not just an anatomical layering, but a functional one, in which cortical (cognitive) processing governs emotional expression. In fact, she nominates Mac-Lean as one origin of a troubling tendency in neuroscientific research to dissociate cognition and emotion: "Because this idea of a brain hierarchy seems intuitively attractive, and because the brain anatomy seems to correspond to a neat and rigid escalation in abilities, scientists and nonscientists alike have accepted for decades the paradigm that emotion and logical thinking—so-called cognitive processes—can be segregated" (5).

However, MacLean's model is more careful than Greenfield implies. What MacLean promotes is a complex set of relations among three neural formations. His claim that each evolutionary formation has "its own special intelligence, its own subjectivity, its own sense of time and space, and its own memory, motor, and other functions" (1990, 9) suggests more than a conventional hierarchical structure. Each part of this triune structure has its own particular disposition, and these dispositions are not arranged in functional hierarchies (in which higher parts dominate the lower). The triune model neither promulgates a rigid hierarchical structure (cognition over emotion; mammalian over reptilian), nor does it disperse these elements into a structureless association (in which we cannot tell the difference between cognitive and emotional responses). What is attractive in MacLean's model is its ability to deploy a conventional hierarchy ("three-brains-in-one") to twist or fold or reticulate the relations among each formation. Suppression is only one, and not the most important, of the relations that might exist among these neural structures. There are ongoing communications among the triune assemblages: MacLean understands them to be "intermeshing" and cofunctioning systems. They operate "somewhat independently" (9), but not, as some have concluded, as autonomous entities.

It is MacLean's empirical work that most carefully demonstrates how the human reptilian formation and its relation to sibling structures might be differently understood. MacLean has been engaged in an enormous body of comparative neurobiological research on extinct and extant reptiles, all of which attempts to make a case for the complex kinship of reptilian and mammalian capacities. For example, he has investigated the paleobiology of therapsids, extinct mammal-like reptiles that predated the dinosaurs and are thought to have been the crucial evolutionary branch linking stem reptiles to modern marsupials and placental mammals. These creatures had skeletal structures (particularly the skull) that approximated mammalian form, and there is some evidence to suggest that they may have behaved in ways identifiably mammalian (e.g., parental care). For MacLean, therapsids are not so much the missing link between reptiles and mammals (thus simply instantiating conventional notions of lineage or intermediate form); they are more like a kind of biological Rosetta stone by which the present-day commerce among vertebrates is made legible. As with Sacks's examples of the bodig patient and branchial myoclonus, MacLean's therapsids make manifest the extensive, constitutive communications of form and function among species and among classes. Crucially, these communications are not simply hierarchical, or suppressive; oftentimes, they breach established evolutionary lines of descent.

One of the most pressing concerns that feminists (from Darwin's time to the present) have had with evolutionary theory is its conventional hierarchical structure: the lower and more primitive species are said to form the base from which the higher and more civilized species arise. Once evolutionary processes are formulated in these terms, all the contentious implications of evolutionary theory (racism, sexism, phylogenetic determinism, social Darwinism) seem to follow naturally, and evolutionary theories become unpalatable for feminism. It has been my argument here that MacLean and Sacks instantiate evolutionary processes differently. Without jettisoning hierarchy entirely (for it remains a powerful conceptual device), MacLean and Sacks amplify the relations that exist across evolutionary branches. This attempt to keep both hierarchical and transversive relations in play dislodges hierarchy from the center of evolutionary explanations. Sacks's and MacLean's models of consanguinity between lower and higher are deconstructive, in the truest sense: they refract, bend, and stress hierarchical relations but without attempting to destroy them and without yearning for a conceptual space beyond them. It is MacLean's struggle to both demarcate a triune structure and keep these tripartite elements in touch with one another in myriad transversive ways that I think is instructive for feminists as they become more interested in the conceptual contributions that could be gleaned from biological knowledges. As a way of underscoring the framework of differentiation and consanguinity I have opened up here via Sacks and MacLean, and before moving to the question of affect in contemporary neuroscience, let me detour through Darwin, *The Origin of Species*, and his experiments with worms.

Evolution as Differentiation

The Origin of Species contains a remarkable account of differentiation of form. There is no pregiven identity of form or function to be found anywhere in nature, Darwin argues; rather, there is mutation, inconstancy, and interconnectivity. *The Origin of Species* is not concerned with biological origins as we would normally think of them today (e.g., the origin of life; the transition from inorganic to organic molecular structures). Rather, as the title makes plain, *The Origin of Species* is interested in biological differentiation (speciation): How do creatures get to be different? And how do different bodily forms relate?

Gillian Beer's (1996a, 1996b, 2000) canonical work on Darwin provides a compelling and lucid account of differentiation in Darwin's theory of evolution. Though not explicitly feminist, Beer's readings of Darwin nonetheless provide a framework for using evolutionary theory to rethink key political issues concerning embodiment, intersubjectivity, and human culture. Differentiation is at the center of this rethinking: "This emphasis on slight differences, deviations, rather than approximation to the parent type, is among the most profound of Darwin's challenges to conventional thinking. Not the normative but difference proves to be the generative principle" (1996a, xx–xxi). Beer understands evolutionary systems after Darwin to be about more than lines of descent: "Evolutionary theory created a system which could not be resolved into a simple mathematical elegance. Profusion is a necessary component of its explanation. Selection is crucial also but it is a selection relying on hyperproductivity, upon a fertility beyond use or number" (2000, 12–13). In a similar vein, Elizabeth Grosz (1999) makes explicit the value of Darwin for contemporary feminist concerns: "[Darwin's] work is not 'feminist' in any sense, but as a profound and complex account of the organic becoming of matter, of the strategies of survival and multiplication of these becomings in the face of the obstacles or problems of existence that life poses for them, it is or should be of some direct interest and value for feminism" (42). This section attempts a specific reading of Darwin's interest in multiplication and differentiation.

Darwin's inquiry into the origin of species (how one species evolves out of and into another) leads him to dispute the conventional demarcation of species as groups separated by sterility (conventionally, species are defined by their inability to interbreed, whereas varieties or subspecies are defined by their ability to interbreed). Throughout the *Origin* Darwin shows that not only can some varieties not interbreed, but some species can: "It can thus be shown that neither sterility nor fertility affords any clear distinction between species and varieties" (1859, 201). His point is not that there has been a misclassification or an error in regard to particular groups; rather,

Darwin argues that the possibility of dividing biological groups according to fertile or infertile affinities is not structurally possible. In this way, the conventional notion that a biological identity (species) is fixed through a circumscription of sexual or reproductive influence is disputed by Darwin; reproduction and fertility become more comprehensive events. That is, the Darwinian system is a system of generalized fertility: it is the differentiating affinity of biological matter (of organism with organism, of organ with organ) that is the basis of evolutionary effects. This is not a benign ecological interactivity, or a direct descent, where entities cohabit and breed only with their own. The Darwinian world is constituted through fierce reciprocation, in which there is active commerce among species, between kingdoms, between organic and inorganic forms, among biology and geology and culture and psychology. In this Darwinian system, everything touches and interbreeds with everything else: "The structure of every organic being is related, in the most essential yet often hidden manner, to that of all other organic beings, with which it comes into competition for food or residence, or from which it has to escape, or on which it preys" (64).

This system of generative differentiation is nowhere better demonstrated than in Darwin's last book, on the vegetable mold and the action of worms. Perhaps the most remarkable claim of the book is near the beginning: "I was thus led to conclude that all the vegetable mould [the fine layer of fertile soil that covers the surface of every temperate country] over the whole country has passed many times through, and will again pass many times through, the intestinal canals of worms" (1881, 4). That is, what comes to be the vegetable mold is such only after its digestion and excretion through animal bodies. With this simple observation, Darwin enacts a transposition that inverts the conventional relation of the animal and plant kingdoms, the organic and inorganic realms, and the human and worm worlds. And he marks the first of these transpositions rhetorically: even though the mold consists essentially of vegetable and inorganic matter, Darwin suggests that the term "animal mold" would be a more appropriate term for the substance at hand.

From this initial observation about the animality of the soil, Darwin builds up a richly reciprocative natural world. What he has observed is not a simple passage of vegetable through animal, but a complex system of digestion: everything is being eaten, consumed, incorporated, and excreted. For example, worm digestion itself is not a closed biological system: worms don't eat just vegetation, as Darwin found out in his many potted experiments in his dining room; worms eat meat and fat and sugar and cardboard and licorice and also each other ("They are cannibals, for the two halves of a dead worm placed in two of the pots were dragged into burrows and gnawed," 37). Moreover, digestion begins well before the worm actually ingests food: leaves are moistened and softened with intestinal secretions.

The result is that leaves are partially digested before they are taken into the alimentary canal, a process Darwin calls "extra-stomachal digestion" (44). One of the peculiar aspects of worm digestion is that they ingest the vegetable mold for both nutritive and geological reasons. Worm castings are thrown up at the mouths of burrows, Darwin observes, both as a result of eating (the taking in of nourishment) and as a result of digging (the construction of burrows). That is, the vegetable mold is received alternately as organic and inorganic substance within the worm's alimentary canal. Darwin leaves unaddressed the question of how this differentiated relation to the soil is enacted, as if he understands that the difference between the biological and the mineral is an ongoing negotiation.

Belatedly, even man figures in this worm world. In the final paragraph of the book, as Darwin contemplates the beauty of a smooth turf-covered expanse, man's puny efforts in relation to the vegetable mold are noted: "The plough is one of the most ancient and most valuable of man's inventions; but long before he existed the land was in fact regularly ploughed, and still continues to be thus ploughed by earth-worms" (316).[7] In a move that marks so much of his work, Darwin simultaneously builds and collapses hierarchies: man above worm; worm above man; vegetable inside animal; animal inside vegetable; incorporation, then digestion; digestion, then incorporation. Throughout the text, he emphasizes the tremendous influence of worms on the earth: "It may be doubted whether there are many other animals which have played so important a part in the history of the world, as have these lowly creatures" (316). "In his characteristically modest way," Adam Phillips notes, "Darwin is shuffling the traditional hierarchies; not cutting men down to size, like an arrogant deity, but trying to get them the right size" (1999, 50).

It is for these reasons (the intuitive shuffling of hierarchical relations; the intuitive interfacing of different embodied modalities; the attention to transversing connections) that Sacks and MacLean are Darwinians of the most faithful kind. In an environment in which neo-Darwinian commentaries have come to dominate what can be said under the name Darwin, it becomes difficult to hear how evolutionary arguments may be politically, methodologically, or conceptually useful for feminism (Angier 1999). Evolutionary psychology has become a particularly toxic antifeminist, antiqueer mode of neo-Darwinism commentary; much of its success can be attributed to how it shuts down (or renders illegible) other modes of reading evolution in the popular and scientific domains. The evolutionary work of the feminist primatologists (e.g., Haraway 1989; Hrdy 1981, 2000; Morgan 1997) has been a notable exception to this tendency for neo-Darwinism to collapse into political conventionalism. With careful attention to empirical detail, these feminists have been able to form a robust alliance between feminism and primatology, an alliance that neither indulges feminist conventions nor acquiesces to scientific authority, but instead builds a domain of knowledge that is legible and credible in both feminist and scientific terms. I want to push the uses of evolution in another direction. In Paul MacLean and Oliver Sacks we have neuroscientists who have been able to mobilize evolutionary arguments in ways that are not only transformative of conventional neo-Darwinian expectations, but that extend our critical concerns beyond the mammalian. And they place differentiation and the interfacing of different materialities at the fore of their models. As such, they offer invaluable tools for feminism as it engages more deeply with biological or geological or neurological or physical models of the world.

Emotional Lizards

Despite the prominence of emotion in late nineteenth-century science (Darwin, James) and the neurological training of some of the nineteenth century's preeminent psychologists (Freud, Hughlings-Jackson), twentieth-century neurology turned its back on the study of emotion. Reviewing Joseph LeDoux's (1996) book *Emotional Brain*, which marks a return in neuroscientific research to the question of emotion, Antonio Damasio muses that "we may never understand why emotion was given the cold shoulder of science for almost 100 years" (1997, 117). Of course, feminism may be able to provide Damasio with some working hypotheses: the long-standing preference in scientific endeavor for cognitive, rational, and conscious events, and the corresponding distaste for emotional and bodily states. Damasio bumps into such a hypothesis when he declares that the body is "probably the central issue in the neurobiology of emotion" (117).

In ways that would have seemed highly unlikely as recently as the 1980s, there has been a remarkable turnaround in neuroscientific interest in emotion. It was Damasio's (1994) *Descartes' Error* that brought this transformation to a mainstream audience. His central contribution was to alert his audience, via neuroscientific data, to the central role emotion plays in rationality: "Reason may not be as pure as most of us think it is or wish it were . . . emotions and feelings may not be intruders in the bastion of reason at all: they may be enmeshed in its networks, for worse *and* for better" (xii). That this renewed interest in emotion was apposite in general cultural terms was confirmed by the enthusiastic reception given to Daniel Goleman's (1995) bestseller, *Emotional Intelligence*. LeDoux's book *Emotional Brain* brings similar questions of emotion and neurology to a popular, nonspecialist audience. His research locates affect within the confines of evolutionary constraints (especially as this links human emotions to emotions in animals); it is for this reason that I focus on LeDoux here.[8]

LeDoux's approach to the neurology of emotion is unmistakably reductionist: "I view emotions as biological functions of the nervous system . . . The brain systems that generate emotional behaviors are highly conserved through many levels of evolutionary history" (1996, 12, 17). There is, for LeDoux, a phylogenetic link between human neural-emotional structures and those of the lower animals. For example, there has been little change, he argues, from stem reptiles to mammals in terms of the behavior and physiology of fear. Disregarding MacLean's distinction between the reptilian and the emotional, LeDoux suggests that "in some ways we are emotional lizards" (174). At first blush, LeDoux's work may seem incompatible with critical concerns, or perhaps even antagonistic toward them. The association of emotionality with the reptilian could set afloat a whole raft of problematic conceptual associations: emotion, nature, female, primitives. I hope that by this point in the chapter, a different way of reading reptilianism in relation to emotions may seem possible. However, in this final section I would like to focus on something different. I am interested in the theory of differentiated affect that LeDoux champions, the critique of cognitive primacy that such a theory advances, and how he integrates this with a schema of differentiated neural pathways for the affects. These aspects of LeDoux's approach to neurology, evolution, and affect, even if they are unevenly articulated, may be of some interest to broader theoretical debates about the relation of soma and psyche. I argue (following the counsel of Sedgwick and Frank, 1995) that not only is this differential approach to the affects a paradigm shift for contemporary critical theories, it is an approach that needs to be accessed through close engagement with biological and evolutionary data.

Let me back up a little. Scientific theories of emotion since Darwin have fallen into two broad camps. Darwin (1872) argued that there are a small number of discrete, basic emotions in humans (e.g., fear, shame, joy, anger) that have been phylogenetically preserved and some of which are "the direct result of the constitution of the nervous system" (66). This has been called a categorical theory of the emotions, in which the differences among, say, fear, shame, joy, and anger are formulated as a function of bioevolutionary constraints. Despite the extensive citational use made of Darwin in scientific texts on emotion, most scientific (especially psychological) research on emotion in the twentieth century employed quite a different model. This second model, a cognitively oriented one, is best exemplified by the canonical work of Schacter and Singer (1962). It is hypothesized in this model that emotion is a function of arousal and cognition: once physiologically aroused, we label states of arousal "fear" or "shame" or "joy" or "anger" on the basis of the physical and social cues available to us. In this model, cognition "exerts a steering function" (380); different emotions are the effect of different cognitive appraisals of an aroused condition.[9]

Emphasizing the biophenomenological immediacy of the affects, rather than their digression through cognitive mechanisms of evaluation, Sedgwick and Frank (1995) debunk this appraisal model brilliantly: "So ask yourself this: how long does it take you, after being awakened in the night by (a) a sudden noise, or (b) sexual arousal, to cognitively 'analyze' and 'appraise' 'the current state of affairs' well enough to assign the appropriate quale to your emotion? That is, what is the temporal lag from the moment of sleep interruption to the ('subsequent') moment when you can judge whether what you're experiencing is luxuriation or terror?" (19).

In his 1996 book, LeDoux launches a similarly strong attack on cognitivist approaches to emotion: "My desire to protect emotion from being consumed by the cognitive monster comes from my understanding of how emotion is organized in the brain" (68–69). "Cognitive monster" is an unusually strong and unusually colloquial turn of phrase for a neurologist, even in a popular scientific publication; it speaks to the depth of feeling that has come to structure this ongoing theoretical and empirical debate about the nature of emotion and its relation to other psychological and biological systems.[10] LeDoux is keen to position emotions as psychological events that cannot be devolved to cognitive mechanisms. What is interesting for my purposes is that he builds this argument for the specificity of emotions with recourse to neurological and evolutionary theories. It is through neurological and evolutionary argument that LeDoux is able to (1) differentiate emotions from cognitions and (2) provide a schema for the various affiliations between emotional and cognitive systems. That is, it is through close attention to biological detail that a more expansive theory of affect begins to emerge. Rather than being the knowledges of bedrock against which feminism should agitate, neurobiological and evolutionary research may provide innovative conceptual schemata for understanding emotion.

The neuropsychological data that LeDoux reviews suggest, among other things, that emotion is processed in different ways in the brain from more obviously cognitive tasks; that the first psychological response to a stimulus may be emotional rather than cognitive or appraising;[11] that emotional systems are more intimately connected to bodily sensations than are cognitive systems; and that memories of emotionally significant stimuli and cognitive stimuli are processed differently. In short, he argues, there is very little neurological data to support the thesis that emotion is subordinate to cognition, and there is substantial support for the idea that different kinds of emotions are processed in different ways in the brain.

It is for these reasons that LeDoux is critical of MacLean's notion of the limbic system as the body that mediates affect in the brain. LeDoux argues that there isn't a single neurological system (not anatomically, not functionally) that superintends all emotional experience. If emotions are categorically differentiated—neurologically and phenomenologically—then one might hypothesize that there is not one emotional/limbic system in the brain, but many (Jaak Panksepp, 1998, for example, makes a case for seven basic neuroemotional systems: seeking, rage, fear, panic, lust, care, play). Theories of interlocking neurological modules and systems have come to replace conventional theories of neurological location and segregation: the brain is thought of as "a collection of systems, sometimes called modules, each with different functions" (LeDoux 1996, 105). The traditional notion that psychological capacities are sequestered in specific areas in the brain (emotion down here, cognition up there) is now widely contested. What becomes conceptually critical in theories of brain function is how such modules connect, amalgamate, and dissociate. LeDoux thinks of different emotions, not as different outputs of a singular system, but as neurologically specific modules that have been fashioned by specific evolutionary pressures: "It is true that at times evolution might act globally, say increasing the size of the entire brain, but by and large most evolutionary changes in the brain take place at the level of individual modules" (105).

This neurobiological formulation of the brain and its emotional systems allows feminists to work much more productively with neurological and evolutionary data. The modularity thesis formulates the emotional and cognitive worlds as a series of interfacing systems. This has a number of important consequences. Not only does it make more dynamic the ontology of emotion (Does fear amplify rage? Under what conditions? When is joy followed by shame and when by fear? What kinds of individuals or groups are more prone to anger?), but also it allows for rich communications and alliances between emotions and cognitions.[12] At times, cognitions (ideologies, belief systems, denials, misrecognitions) may operate to suppress certain emotions, but the possible amalgamations, dissociations, and partial associations between emotions and cognitions are more extensive than this. As modularity and connectivity come to shape the conceptual landscape of the neurosciences, the case for affective profusion, multiplicity of form, and what Beer has called "fertility beyond use or number" begins to override any conventional fondness for strict demarcation of organisms, organs, and psychologies.

I spent some time in the earlier sections of this chapter outlining how such systems of connectivity have been elaborated in models of the reptilian brain, reptilian behavior, and worm ecologies. I stressed how Sacks, MacLean, and Darwin bring analytic attention to systems of consanguinity: paleontology/pathology; fish/reptile/mammal; cortical/subcortical/limbic; worm/human. LeDoux's model of emotions as neuroevolutionary modules fits this same general orientation. The appellation "emotional lizard" might be simply a kind of psychological primitivism (i.e., in certain circumstances we will be reduced to reflexive, prehistoric behavior), but LeDoux occasionally hints at a more complex set of relations between the new and the old, the emotional and the cortical, the reptilian and the mammalian. For example, MacLean's model contends that the limbic system is composed of phylogenetically old cortex that is common to fish, amphibians, reptiles, and birds (thus the label paleomammalian). In this model, the lower vertebrates have only old cortex, but mammals have both old and new cortex. However LeDoux argues that this distinction is by no means clear-cut: "So-called primitive creatures do in fact have areas that meet the structural and functional criteria of neocortex. What had been confusing was that these cortical areas were not exactly in the place that they are in mammals so it was not obvious that they were the same structures. As a result of these discoveries, it is no longer possible to say that some parts of the mammalian cortex were older than other parts. And once the distinction between old and new cortex breaks down, the whole concept of mammalian brain evolution is turned on its head" (1996, 100).

In this chapter I have stressed the inverting and transversing lines of influence in evolutionary models. The organs, organisms, groups, and ecologies that are constituted by evolutionary forces are not simply the effect of hierarchical organization and direct descent. Bodily forms are the product of a widespread commerce among groups, and bodies continue to instantiate and participate in these richly divergent evolutionary relations.

Some researchers have been able to mobilize aspects of evolutionary theory to very effective theoretical and political ends (e.g., the feminist primatologists). I have argued that the potential uses of evolutionary theory may be wider than this. For example, not only might feminism turn evolution on its head (Morgan 1997), but feminist theory may find itself diverted into new conceptual territory by evolutionary models. Theories of the affects that demand attention to neurobiological and evolutionary detail are one such example of this new influence on feminist theories of psyche and soma.

········

Introduction

1. He was probably also finishing off "A Note upon the 'Mystic Writing Pad'" (1925b). See Cilliers (1998) and E. A. Wilson (1996) for analysis of the importance of this paper and Freud's early neurological work for contemporary readings of neuroscience.

2. Freud was notoriously ambivalent about the relationship between psychoanalysis and the biological sciences, and readers of early Freud are likewise divided about whether he abandoned, or simply sublimated, his neurological ambitions (Derrida 1978; Geerardyn 1997; Lane 1994; L. Miller 1991; Pribram and Gill 1976; Sacks 1998b; Solms and Saling 1990; E. A. Wilson 1998). The recent interest in the conjunction of contemporary neuroscience and psychoanalysis continues to debate this issue (Bilder and LeFever 1998; Guttmann and Scholz-Strasser 1999; Kaplan-Solms and Solms 2000; Schore 1999; see also http://www.neuro-psa.com).

3. "I wish to speak of the *impression left* by Freud, by the event which carries this family name, the nearly unforgettable and incontestable, undeniable *impression* (even and above all for those who deny it) that Sigmund Freud will have *made* on anyone, after him, who speaks *of him* or speaks *to him*, and who must then, accepting it or not, knowing it or not, be thus marked . . . In any given discipline, one can no longer, one should no longer be able to, thus one no longer has the right or the means to claim to speak of this without having been marked in advance, in one way or another, by this Freudian impression" (Derrida 1995, 30).

4. For early and influential feminist accounts of hysteria, see Copjec (1987), David-Ménard (1989), Gallop (1982), Grosz (1989), Hunter (1985), Irigaray (1985), and Showalter (1985).

5. It is worth noting that the emerging literature on neuroscience and psychoanalysis is of little help in this regard either. Despite the large body of neuroscientific knowledge available, the biological details of hysteria have yet to be cogently theorized. The centrality of the brain (particularly the cortex) in the neuropsychoanalytic literature shifts the etiology of hysteria from the body to the brain, but it does not explain the mechanisms of conversion at either locale. This relocation has the added disadvantage of limiting the nervous body to the

brain (this difficulty is explored further in chapter 2 in relation to the nervous innervation of the gut).

6. The general argument that Showalter presents in *The Female Malady* (1985) is also reproduced in her most recent work on hysteria (1997).

7. In this respect, Oliver Sacks's (1995, 1996) neurologically informed stories give a more acute understanding of the psychology of color vision. I return to the usefulness of Sacks's work for reading neurology in chapter 5.

8. There were two important bodily connections between Freud and Fraulein Elisabeth. First, Freud had dispensed with hypnosis by this time, but was still pressing his hands on the head of his patients: "The idea occurred to me of resorting to the device of applying pressure to the head . . . I carried this out by instructing the patient to report to me faithfully whatever appeared before her inner eye or passed through her memory at the moment of pressure" (Breuer and Freud 1895, 145). Second, Freud had suffered from the same kind of muscular pain that he was treating in Fraulein Elisabeth: "In 1895 [Freud published] a paper on an unusual compression neuropathy (meralgia paresthetica)—resulting in pain and sensitivity in the thigh—a condition he himself suffered from, and which he had observed in several patients under his care" (Sacks 1998a, 122).

9. V. S. Ramachandran's experiments with phantom limbs demonstrate one way the body so folds, maps, and relocates itself (Ramachandran and Blakeslee 1998). Some patients with phantom limbs report that the missing limb is mapped onto another part of the body (e.g., a missing hand often maps onto the skin of the face; a missing foot often maps onto the genitals). If the map on the face is stimulated, the patient experiences sensation in the phantom hand; likewise, sex may make a phantom foot itchy. Ramachandran explains these phenomena with reference to the sensory homunculus: feet and genitals, hands and faces are represented in adjacent areas on the cortex; stimulation of genitals or the skin on the face seems to activate sensations in the neighboring hands or feet. The tendency to explain these kinds of somatic phenomena ("Eureka! The mystery is solved," 38) with reference only to the cortex short-circuits a more expansive understanding of the data, not only in terms of the body but also in terms of the rest of the nervous system. Nevertheless, Ramachandran's data give us a glimpse of the body in conversation with itself.

10. Vicki Kirby alerted me to the usefulness of this seemingly antiquated formulation. See Kirby (1997) for a meticulous reading of the remarkable substrate of the hysterical body.

1   *Freud, Prozac, and Melancholic Neurology*

1. For example, in her 1995 review of *Listening to Prozac* Judith Kegan Gardiner suggests that Kramer is advocating a fairly straightforward version of biological determinism: "He claims [Prozac] does more than restore sick people to their former selves; it makes them 'better than well' and so proves the dominance of biological over psychological forces in determining personality" (503). Similarly: "Kramer believes that Prozac proves psychoanalysis to be wrong in attributing adult misery to childhood psychological trauma. Instead, he prefers biological, even evolutionary arguments about the functions of mood and chemicals in the brain" (505–506). What strikes me as interesting in this assessment (which I take to be typical of many feminist responses to *Listening to Prozac*; see also Griggers 1997 and Zita 1998) is the way Kramer's biologism can be so readily determined. If, as Gardiner claims, "biological and social aspects of human personality are mutually constitutive" (512), why is Kramer's text not taken to be a particularly arresting account of such mutual constitution? Is it that Gardiner (like so many feminists) is able to allow this constitutive effect to flow only one way: from the social to the biological? Why is it that an account of mutual

constitution cannot be sustained with biological, even evolutionary arguments? After all, isn't evolutionary theory an account of the mutual constitution of the organism and environment? (This claim is argued in depth in chapters 4 and 5.) In such critical moments feminism's commitment to a position of *mutual* constitution becomes specious, and this mode of feminist analysis falls back into a cultural determinism that is as narrow as the biological determinism it claims to contest. What I hope to demonstrate in my reading of *Listening to Prozac* is that Kramer presents a thesis of mutual constitution that is profoundly enabling for feminist politics.

2. "It is difficult to make any statement of general validity about neurasthenia, so long as we use that name to cover all the things which Beard has included under it. In my opinion, it can be nothing but a gain to neuropathology if we make an attempt to separate from neurasthenia proper all those neurotic disturbances in which, on the one hand, the symptoms are more firmly linked to one another than to the typical symptoms of neurasthenia (such as intercranial pressure, spinal irritation, and dyspepsia with flatulence and constipation); and which, on the other hand, exhibit essential differences in their aetiology and mechanism from the typical neurasthenic neurosis" (Freud 1895b, 90).

3. This hypothesis covers only the cases of acquired neurasthenia, where heredity or family disposition can be ruled out as the cause of nervous weakness: "It may be taken as a recognized fact that *neurasthenia* is a frequent consequence of an abnormal sexual life. The assertion, however, which I wish to make and to test by my observations is that neurasthenia is always *only* a sexual neurosis" (Freud 1893, 179).

4. "The problems of the 'actual' neuroses, whose symptoms are probably generated by direct toxic damage, offer psycho-analysis no points of attack. It can do little towards throwing light on them and must leave the task to biologico-medical research" (Freud 1916, 389).

5. In his foreword to *Living with Prozac* (Elfenbein 1995), Kramer nominates confidence, flexibility, resilience, and assertiveness as the effects that Prozac can have on melancholic temperament. I want to attribute to neurology itself the same kind of robust structure. Too often, it seems, neurology is thought to be autocratic, rigid, patriarchal. Both Freud and Kramer have a more attuned, empathic relation to neurology.

6. Derrida has already commented on Freud's particularly cogent use of metaphor (here, in relation to the metaphorics of writing): "Freud, no doubt, is not manipulating metaphors, if to manipulate a metaphor means to make of the known an allusion to the unknown. On the contrary, through the insistence of his metaphoric investment he makes what we believe we know under the name writing enigmatic" (1978, 199).

7. Although the stress of electrical current and the stress of psychological trauma are different in nature, they may be similar in their neuropsychological effects. Kramer (1993) discusses experimental evidence that suggests that a psychological trauma can cause changes in the endocrine system, such that the brain itself is rewired. These stressors "can cause chemical and anatomical changes whose behavioral effects may not be apparent for some time" (118). Sexual abuse is one form of such stress in humans. Kramer cites a study by the U.S. National Institutes of Mental Health that points to the effect of childhood sexual abuse on stress-hormone systems. In a four- to five-year period following sexual abuse, girls who had been subjected to this abuse had higher than normal cortisol levels compared to a matched sample. Moreover, these disruptions to the stress-hormone system were highly correlated to depression. Kramer hypothesizes that the original trauma may itself not be causing depression, but may be rendering these girls more susceptible to depression from that point on. A similar conceptual model has already been elucidated by Freud under the name *Nachträglichkeit*, deferred action. The emerging psychoanalytically inclined literature on the neurobiology of trauma (e.g., Schore 1999) supports this kind of model of psyche-soma relations.

8. Of course, it is also credible to argue that these symptoms originate in cultural dysfunction. Indeed, both Griggers (1997) and Zita (1998) chastise Kramer for his failure to identify the cultural structures that generate and maintain depression in women: "Kramer and other proponents of biopsychiatry do not see the alteration of the body's memories as suppression of the history and experiential reality of particular social groups that may have a detrimental effect on the long-term healing process of that group" (Griggers 1997, 132); "While Kramer raises such [cultural] concerns in *Listening to Prozac,* he fails to follow their implications once the smiling and happy faces of his chemically 'born again' clients line up against the hesitations of his second thoughts" (Zita 1998, 70). It is often the case that commentaries that insist on the dominance of cultural analysis of depression belittle the importance of interventions along different axes (the intrapsychic, the microbiological) and according to different chronologies (in this lifetime; preferably in the next few weeks). It is my argument that these kinds of intervention are not only legitimate, they are indispensable. Here I, too, pay little attention to cultural concerns. I take this position to divert critical attention—just for a minute—to the advantages of neurological analyses of depression and neurasthenia.

9. Moreover, any attribution of an antipsychological or antipsychoanalytic agenda to Kramer should be demolished by his subsequent book (Kramer 1997b), which is grounded in a traditional (i.e., nonbiological) psychotherapeutic literature.

10. One definition of determination offered by the Oxford English Dictionary is "The determining of bounds or fixing of limits; delimitation; definition; a fixing of the extent, position, or identity (of anything)."

11. The autobiographical literature about taking Prozac reflects this variance (Elfenbein 1995; Slater 1998; Wurtzel 1995). See Metzl (2001) for a careful and refreshing analysis of the narrative structures that govern these autobiographical accounts.

12. Jacqueline Zita's (1998) analysis of Kramer, Prozac, and feminism pushes neurological detail to one side. Much of the biochemical detail about fluoxetine hydrochloride is contained in footnotes, as if it is auxiliary to any criticism that will be developed. Hewitt, Fraser, and Berger (2000) are more explicit: "An account of how Prozac affects the neurotransmission process is beyond the scope of this essay, and in many respects quite beside the point" (164). Perhaps one of the most remarkable details in Zita's impeccably researched article is hidden away in a footnote and receives no critical attention: "Serotonin is found in the serum, the intestinal mucosa, and the central nervous system; only 1–2 percent of the body's serotonin is found in the brain" (236). Zita focuses her resistance to Prozac on the central nervous system, yet 98 percent of the drug is elsewhere. The importance of the intestinal mucosa for readings of depression, neurology, and the body is explored in the next chapter.

2   The Brain in the Gut

1. "I did not carry the analysis of the symptoms far enough" (Breuer and Freud 1895, 48). More worrying, Freud's hypnotic interventions seem to have produced a long-lasting attenuation of Frau Emmy's memory: "My energy [in eliminating traumatic memories] seems to have carried me too far. When, as much as eighteen months later, I saw Frau Emmy in a relatively good state of health, she complained that there were a number of important moments in her life of which she had only the vaguest memory" (61).

2. Breuer and Freud (1895) think of hysterical symptoms as "the effects and residues of excitations which have acted upon the nervous system as traumas" (86). Such residues are left when the original excitation (trauma) has not been adequately discharged (abreacted). They divide the nervous effects of hysteria into two: those played out in the psychic sphere,

and those transformed into somatic symptoms. In the case of conversion hysteria, undischarged excitation has been transformed into somatic symptoms. Freud diagnoses Frau Emmy as hysterical, but he notes that there is very little in the way of conversion in her case. Gastric pain (the residue of excitation on the enteric nervous system) seems to be one of the few events of conversion in Frau Emmy's case. Instead, her condition is marked primarily by animal phobias, abulia (inhibition of will), and alterations in mood (anxiety and melancholia). By and large, the original excitation has not been transformed into somatic symptoms, but has remained in the psychic sphere in the form of delusions and disturbances to mood. Her mixed hysterical symptomology documents the traffic between psychic and somatic domains: how psychic afflictions (abulia, melancholia) and somatic afflictions (gastric pain) are affiliated and how a treatment of her symptoms may require intervention at those sites where these psychic-somatic affiliations are most intense (e.g., the epigastrium).

3. I have used Appenzeller and Oribe (1997), Furness (2000), Furness and Costa (1987), Gariepy (2001), Gershon (1998), Goyal and Hirano (1996), Kim and Camilleri (2000), Talley (2001), Woods, Alpers, and Andrews (1999), the September 1999 issue of *Gut* (volume 45, supplement II) on "Rome II: A Multinational Consensus on Functional Gastrointestinal Disorders," the December 2000 issue of *Gut* (volume 47, supplement IV) on "The Enteric Nervous System in Health and Disease," and the British Society of Gastroenterology guidelines for the management of irritable bowel syndrome (Jones et al. 2000) to construct the analysis of the enteric nervous system that follows.

4. The vertebrate nervous system can be divided into the central nervous system (the brain and spinal cord) and the peripheral nervous system (see figure 5). The peripheral nervous system is usually said to comprise the somatic nervous system (which relays afferent sensory information to the CNS and efferent innervation to the body's voluntary muscles) and the autonomic nervous system, which controls the muscles of the internal organs (viscera) and the glands. The organs that the ANS regulates are thought to function involuntarily and out of conscious awareness (e.g., the heart), even though some ANS functions can be brought under conscious control. Conventionally, the ANS has been said to contain two subdivisions: the sympathetic and parasympathetic. This division of the ANS was supported by anatomical considerations (the nerve fibers of the sympathetic system originate in the middle of the spinal cord, the thoracic and lumbar regions; the nerve fibers of the parasympathetic system originate in the top and bottom of the spinal cord, the cranial and sacral regions), and by the biochemical thesis that each branch had its own specific neuro-

Figure 5. Organization of the vertebrate nervous system.

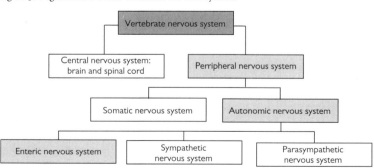

transmitter: norepinephrine (or noradrenaline, as it is called outside the United States) in the sympathetic branch, and acetylcholine in the parasympathetic branch. Speaking broadly, the sympathetic system innervates "fight or flight" responses (increased heartbeat, fast and shallow breathing, tense muscles), whereas the parasympathetic system regulates "rest and digest" responses (slower heartbeat, slow and deep inhalation and expiration, relaxed muscles).

5. This recent research, which expanded rapidly in the 1990s, revivifies a body of experimental data gathered in the late nineteenth and early twentieth centuries. In 1899 William Bayliss and Ernest Starling published data about the peristaltic reflex in the gut of dogs and noted that this action (which they named "the law of the intestine") was intrinsic to the gut. Rather than being under the direct control of the CNS (as all peripheral nervous action was thought to be), the peristaltic reflex was regulated by the gut itself. When Bayliss and Starling severed the nerves between the gut and the CNS, the peristaltic reflex remained intact: "Since a reflex behavior could thus be elicited in segments of the bowel after all input from the brain or spinal cord had been eliminated, Bayliss and Starling attributed the 'law of the intestine' to what they called the 'local nervous mechanism' of the gut" (Gershon 1998, 5). The two major neural webs that form this local nervous mechanism, the myenteric (Meissner's) plexus and the submucosa (Auerbach's) plexus, had been mapped out already in the mid–nineteenth century. This nineteenth-century research laid the groundwork for thinking of the enteric neurons as a distinct nervous system. In his landmark 1921 text on the autonomic nervous system, John Langley saw clear evidence for considering the enteric nerves to be a separate autonomic system: "I have placed [the cells of Auerbach's and Meissner's plexuses] in a class by themselves as the enteric nervous system. This classification is, I think, still advisable, for the central connexion of the enteric nerve cells is still uncertain, and evidence has been obtained that they have automatic and reflex functions which other peripheral nerve cells do not possess" (9). Langley therefore divided the ANS into three branches: the sympathetic, the parasympathetic, and the enteric. According to Gershon (1998), this taxonomy lay fallow until interest in the ENS was rejuvenated in the 1960s. Today it is still common to see introductory texts on the ANS refer only to the sympathetic and parasympathetic branches.

6. Gershon (1999) notes that "species differences have been found in the chemical coding of enteric nerve cells, so observations made in guinea pigs cannot be directly applied to rodents and certainly not to humans" (35). The guinea pig (and other rodents) has been one of the most commonly used experimental animals in research on the ENS. A complete map of the neurons in the small intestine of the guinea pig has now been completed (Furness 2000).

7. There is a substantial body of research on serotonin and vomiting (emesis) in relation to chemotherapy treatments. Chemotherapy irritates the enterochromaffin cells in the gut mucosa that contain most of the ENS serotonin. These cells release serotonin and this serotonin activates 5-hydroxytryptamine-3 (5-HT3) receptors that have a neuronal connection with the centers in the brain that regulate vomiting. When too much serotonin is released into the gut, consequent to chemotherapy treatments, the vomiting center in the brain is overstimulated, and this contributes to ongoing nausea and vomiting. Serotonin antagonists (that block the 5-HT3 receptor sites and so dampen down stimulation of the higher centers) have been used to help control the vomiting and nausea produced by chemotherapy.

8. Powley (2000), for example, disputes the depiction of the ENS as a second, independent brain. He contends that such an understanding of the ENS has been based on inconclusive data. Using tracer studies, Powley has been able to elucidate extensive anatomical connec-

tion between the ENS and the CNS: "This circuitry suggests that the ENS and CNS are welded together in a neural network in which outflow from the CNS may have pervasive effects on ENS operations, and the ENS may have extensive inputs to the CNS by way of the vagal afferents" (IV32). See also Lundgren (2000) and S. Miller (2000).

9. The Strachey translation of the Fliess correspondence (volume 1 of the *Standard Edition*) mistranslates *Aufstoßen* as flatulence.

10. "The common feature of the Somatoform Disorders is the presence of physical symptoms that suggest a general medical condition (hence the term *somatoform*) and are not fully explained by a general medical condition, by the direct effects of a substance, or by another mental disorder (e.g., Panic Disorder). The symptoms must cause clinically significant distress or impairment in social, occupational, or other areas of functioning. In contrast to Factitious Disorders and Malingering, the physical symptoms are not intentional (i.e., under voluntary control)" (American Psychiatric Association 1994, 445). Somatoform disorders include somatization disorder, hypochondrias, and bodily dysmorphic disorders.

11. It should be noted that Talley's (2001) review suggests that the treatment of IBS using serotonin receptor (5-HT3 and 5-HT4) modulators remains equivocal: "Data for the newer serotonergic agents, reviewed here, suggest that this class of drugs will not become the first-line therapy in IBS, and toxicity has clouded the future of 5HT3 antagonists. However, if these drugs do reach clinical practice they will probably have a place in symptomatic management, and may be better taken on demand rather than as a maintenance therapy" (2066). The practice of drugs being taken "on demand" points again to the transferential aspects of IBS treatment.

12. Drossman (1999) makes this explicit in relation to the Rome II criteria of functional gastrointestinal disorders: "Although psychosocial disturbances can affect the onset, course and outcome of FGIDS . . . they are not required for diagnosis" (II2).

13. See chapter 1, n. 5.

14. Those researchers who do study the connection between affect and neurobiology (e.g., Damasio 1994, 1999; LeDoux 1996; Panksepp 1998) tend to emphasize the biology of emotions rather than the affectivity of biology. They postulate biological bases for emotions, yet these emotions and their biological foundations are constrained by cognitive considerations of efficacy and fitness. Conventional evolutionary explanations of the neurology of emotion take pride in the efficiency of evolutionary outcomes; there is little interest in the exuberant affiliations of evolutionary processes. Somewhat depressingly, emotions explained through conventional evolutionary schemata always seem to make good sense. Richard Doyle's (see 2003) work has been uniquely instructive for me on this point. Chapter 4 in this book uses Darwin to explore the affectivity of neurophysiology; chapter 5 maps some unconventional evolutionary affiliations.

15. This, no doubt, requires more extensive argumentation, which would draw me too far away from questions of the gut. I am referring here to the emergence of contemporary scientific psychology (which these days is almost entirely a science of cognitive processing) out of the so-called cognitive revolution of the 1960s. The computational modeling of cognition has been the means by which psychology, as a discipline, has been able to integrate itself into the scientific mainstream. But this epistemological path has produced oddly bloodless accounts of psychology. Many psychologists at the periphery of their discipline's authority (social psychologists, developmental psychologists, critical psychologists) have commented on how psychological theories often lack an awareness of social contextualization. Perhaps more curiously, these theories also often lack any biological contextualization. Connectionist theories of cognition, for example, have prospered in psychology even though they are neurobiologically implausible.

16. I am not suggesting that the treatment of FGIDs requires the literal laying on of hands, or that psychotherapeutic treatments should take precedence over biomedical ones. Rather, I use this vignette from Freud to focus on how the gut is a psychological organ and on how the psyche is distributed in different somatic-neurological forms (not all of which are contained to the one body: see the analysis of Fraulein Elisabeth in the introduction). Freud would eventually be able to intervene into bodily dysfunction verbally (e.g., Dora's tussis nervosa). My argument is that before psychoanalysis became more conceptually and technically sophisticated, the somatic aspects of transference were more available—to the patient, to the clinician, and to the cultural critic.

17. On occasion, these kinds of enterological states are hinted at. Emeran Mayer comments in the 2001 edition of the newsletter of the International Federation of Functional Gastrointestinal Disorders that the gut is affectively differentiated: "The emotion of fear is associated with inhibition of upper GI (stomach and duodenum) contractions and secretions, and with stimulation of lower GI (sigmoid colon and rectum) motility and secretions. The former may contribute to a sensation of fullness and lack of appetite, the latter to diarrhea and lower abdominal pain . . . Interestingly, when the emotion shifts to anger, the pattern of upper GI activity is reversed, with stimulation of gastric contractions and acid secretion" (http://www.aboutibs.org/Publications/stress.html). Similarly, Wilhelmsen (2000) notes the different effects of emotion on the gastrointestinal tract: fright and depression are associated with a pallor of the mucosa, reduced acid secretion, and reduced gastric motor activity, whereas anger and resentment are associated with the hyperemia of the mucosa, accelerated acid secretion, and increased motor activity.

18. Here I draw on a notion of self that is articulated in Kohutian self psychology, intersubjective infant development theory (Bowlby 1947, 1980; Stern 1985; Trevarthen 1998), attachment theory (Fonagy 2000), and relational psychoanalysis (Mitchell and Aron, 1999). Speaking broadly, all these theories take relations to others to be central to the development and maintenance of robust self states. Psychopathologies (depressions, narcissistic disorders, dissociative disorders) emerge when the self has been damaged during development and/or traumatized in adulthood. Effective treatment of such conditions requires exploration of how relations to others have been disrupted.

19. Psychoanalytic theories of eating disorders (specifically, anorexia and bulimia) have become more and more interested in the ideational aspects of eating (What does it mean?) and less and less interested in the biological aspects of eating (What happens in the gut?). Bemporad and Herzog (1989) note that to trace the history of psychoanalytic explanations of eating disorders is "almost to follow the historical course of psychoanalysis itself" (1). As psychoanalysis has become more conceptually and technically sophisticated, it has been much less interested in somatic detail. In the 1930s, the Chicago Psychoanalytic Institute embarked on an investigation of the relation between the psyche and "vegetative" (autonomic) systems: circulation, respiration, and endocrinology. Gastrointestinal disturbances were their first object of concern. In these early papers (Alexander 1934; Bacon 1934; Levey 1934; Levine 1934; G. Wilson 1934), psychoanalytic treatments had yet to dissociate themselves from analysis of the autonomic nervous system: "The alimentary tract is a system which the psychic apparatus uses with great predilection to relieve different emotional tensions. The connection between psychic stimuli and physiologic expression is here direct and relatively uncomplicated" (Alexander 1934, 502). This kind of relation ("direct and relatively uncomplicated") is one I explored in chapter 1 under the rubric "actual neurosis." Psychoanalytic interest in the vegetative systems waned quickly; a case history of eating disorders that was read to the Chicago Psychoanalytical Society in 1941 (and which quotes

admiringly from the earlier research on the gastrointestinal tract) is almost entirely pre-occupied with ideational matters: "The most important specific psychodynamism of the vomiting appears to be a symbolic rejection and restitution of the father's phallus, orally incorporated in an attempt to render exclusive her basic passive dependence on the mother" (Masserman 1941, 240). Jean Walton (2002) has remarked on the turn from the specifics of the gut even earlier in psychoanalysis. Miss Louise K is a patient of Wilhelm Stekel, the notoriously misogynist Viennese psychoanalyst. Louise K uses her proximity to others to regulate her bowels. "In the morning, her first thought was: Whom shall I use as a 'purgative' today" (Stekel 1927, in Walton 2002, 78); she seats herself at the breakfast table beside someone in order that the closeness initiate violent movement of her bowels. Walton notes that Stekel's analysis of Louise K eventually loses its focus on the particularity of the gut: "As soon as the psychoanalytic account of a heterosexualization-gone-wrong takes hold, Stekel seems increasingly reluctant, or unable, to explore Louise's complex bowel habits with the same kind of thoroughness that characterized his initial description of them. Finally, in the concluding point-by-point summary of the case, an Oedipal schema takes over completely, and the intestinal aspect of the study drops out altogether" (86).

3 Hypothalamic Preference

1. In this context, the term nucleus refers to an aggregation of nerve cells. Such nuclei (or ganglia) are anatomically distinct areas in the brain and spinal cord. Here, LeVay is refer-ring to nuclei in the human hypothalamus. In conjunction with the endocrine system, the hypothalamic nuclei are thought to be involved in homeostatic regulation (e.g., eating, diurnal rhythms, aggression, sexuality, body temperature).

2. Rahman and Wilson (2003) give an overview of psychobiological research on sexual orien-tation since LeVay's study. There has been no replication of LeVay's findings. There has been some interest in the dimorphism of other hypothalamic nuclei in relation to sexual orienta-tion, and there also seems to be increasing interest in the hypothalamic structures of the brains of transsexuals. Byne et al. (2000) have reported a sexual dimorphism in one of the hypothalamic nuclei LeVay studied, but they did not investigate differences in sexual orien-tation (see n. 10 below).

3. In violation of his own directive, LeVay has been a prolific contributor to the further interpretation of the original data. In 1992 he resigned from his position at the Salk In-stitute, where the hypothalamic research was conducted. He lists the 1991 *Science* report as the second to last of his scientific publications. It was, however, the first study he had conducted on sexuality; his usual area of neurological expertise was the visual cortex (http://hometown.aol.com/slevay). From 1992 onward LeVay commented extensively on the nature and implications of his 1991 study. He has appeared on TV news programs (*MacNeil/Lehrer NewsHour, Primetime Live, Nightline*) and talk shows (*Donahue, Oprah*), he has written a syndicated column for gay newspapers, he has given legal testimony, he has been a presenter for a Channel 4 documentary (*Born That Way?*), he has given lectures to universities and community organizations about the biology of sexual orientation, and he has written two popular nonfiction books and a novel about the scientific context and cultural implications of neurobiological research on sexuality (*The Sexual Brain*, 1993; *Queer Science*, 1996; *Albrick's Gold*, 1997). *Science* and *Nature* also disregarded LeVay's interdiction; they immediately published further commentary and speculation on his data (Barinaga 1991; Maddox 1991).

4. See Byne (1995), De Cecco and Parker (1995), Fausto-Sterling (1992), Murphy (1997), and Stein (1999) for academic critiques that discuss these methodological and conceptual limitations in LeVay's study. Gallagher (1991) and Gessen and McGowan (1992) in *The Advocate* canvas the variety of political/activist responses to LeVay's study.

5. LeVay's most sustained account of his theoretical commitments, in relation to sexuality, is to be found in *Queer Science* (1996), where he makes his partiality for Hirschfeld's sexology explicit: "a profound admiration for the man, his ideas and his cause" (40). However, it is unclear whether Hirschfeld's research helped structure LeVay's original approach to the study of the hypothalamus and sexual orientation, or whether it has been a post hoc theoretical foundation: "LeVay, who is gay, readily acknowledges that at the root of his inquiry into the origins of sexuality was 'just my own gut feeling that I share with, I think, many gay men. It's not a feeling that has much scientific documentation at the moment'" (Gessen and McGowan 1992, 60).

6. The OED cites "reticulate" in the eighteenth century, but it was used most commonly in the nineteenth century in reference to geographical and geological structure: "1833 *Lyell Princ. Geol.* III. 356 The granite, in this locality, often sends forth so many veins as to reticulate the limestone and schist . . . 1871 Alabaster *Wheel of Law*. 252 The numerous canals and branches of the river which reticulate the flat alluvial plain . . . 1876 Page *Adv. Text-bk. Geol.* iii. 54 Showing a thousand reticulating fissures." In these contexts, reticulate seems to mean the secondary differentiation of a uniform surface by branching geological features. Here, I use reticulate more to emphasize the way in which division, specifically dimorphic division, is a constitutive or originary aspect of a networking structure.

7. See Terry (2000) for an excellent analysis of this study and a general discussion of the limitations and implications of using animal data in studies about human sexuality.

8. There has been considerable confusion in the neurobiological literature on sexual orientation about whether or not a homology between these rodent hypothalamic nuclei and human hypothalamic nuclei exists. In the first instance, the naming of these structures has changed over the years. Gorski, Gordon, Shryne, and Southam (1978) reported sex difference in the medial preoptic nucleus of the rat (MPON); this area was significantly larger in male than female rats. This area became known as the sexually dimorphic nucleus of the preoptic area (SDN-POA). Eleven years later, Allen et al. (1989) reported two sexually dimorphic nuclei in the human hypothalamus. They abandoned the idea of a single sexually dimorphic nucleus in the human brain and focused their attention on a group of nuclei, the interstitial nuclei of the anterior hypothalamus, of which they isolated four: INAH 1, 2, 3, 4. Allen at al. found that INAH 2 and INAH 3 were sexually dimorphic (larger in males than in females). The homology between the structures described in the 1978 and 1989 reports is complicated further by Allen et al.'s acknowledgment that "it is unclear which, if either, of the 2 nuclei we found to be sexually dimorphic in the human brain corresponds to the SDN-POA of the rat" (501). They also advise against using the term INAH 1 interchangeably with SDN-POA: "There is presently no indication that INAH 1 is homologous to the SDN-POA of the rat" (503). Nonetheless, two prominent researchers in the field, Swaab and Hofman (1995), have retained the old nomenclature: "The sexually dimorphic nucleus of the preoptic area (SDN-POA) of the hypothalamus, as first described in the rat by Gorski and colleagues, is still the most conspicuous morphological sex difference in the mammalian brain" (266); they equate the SDN-POA with INAH 1. Byne et al. (2000) canvas the possibility that the SDN-POA in the rat may be homologous to INAH 3 in humans. It is by no means clear that similar structures in the rat and human brains are being compared, nor even that the same structure within the human brain is being described in these different papers.

9. All of the homosexual subjects had died of AIDS; six of the heterosexual men and one of the

heterosexual women had died of AIDS. See LeVay (1991, n. 8) for details concerning the causes of death in the other subjects.

10. Volume rather than cell number or cell density was used as the measure of size because of "the difficulty in precisely defining the neurons belonging to INAH 3" (LeVay 1991, 1036). See Allen et al. (1989, 489) for a full description of this measurement technique. Swaab and Hofman (1995) consider that there are difficulties with such a method: "Volume is susceptible to various pre- and post-mortem factors, such as differences in agonal state and fixation time, but also to histological procedures and methods such as section thickness. Therefore it is essential to include data on total cell numbers of hypothalamic nuclei, since this parameter is not influenced by such factors" (266–267).

11. Leaving aside putative sexual dimorphisms in other hypothalamic nuclei (e.g., the suprachiasmatic nucleus), it is still unclear whether there is a sexual dimorphism in the INAH structures that LeVay studied. Swaab's early work on the dimorphism of the SDN-POA/INAH 1 (Swaab and Fliers 1985) initiated much of the interest in the hypothalamus and sex differences. However, this finding has not been replicated by another research group, even though Swaab et al. (2001) claim the sex difference in this area in the rat "is so evident that it can even be observed with the naked eye" (93). Other researchers have reported a sexual dimorphism in INAH 2 or 3, but not in INAH 1.

	INAH 1 (SDN-POA)	INAH 2	INAH 3	INAH 4
Swaab and Fliers 1985	Larger in men	Not studied	Not studied	Not studied
Allen et al. 1989	No sex difference	Larger in men	Larger in men	No sex difference
Hofman and Swaab 1989	Larger in men	Not studied	Not studied	Not studied
LeVay 1991	No sex difference	No sex difference	Larger in men	No sex difference
Byne et al. 2000	No sex difference	No sex difference	Larger in men	No sex difference

12. The template n=2 includes pairs, dimorphisms, divisions, and bilateralities. Think of paired nucleotides and the double helix or lungs and kidneys. Bilaterality is a common organization of human biology: the limbs, the sense organs, the cortical hemispheres are all paired, although they are often asymmetrical. One particularly important mode of bilateral organization of limbs, sense organs, and neurology is the optic chiasma: the crossing of the right optic nerve to the left side of the brain, and the left optic nerve to the right side of the brain.

13. Hegarty (1997) has suggested that LeVay's statistical analysis could have been conducted more rigorously. Hegarty's alternative analysis (which confines itself to the data from subjects who died of AIDS and measures differences across all four INAH volumes) does not register a statistically significant difference in relation to sexual orientation in the volumes of INAH 3. Any body of data can be subject to different batteries of statistical testing, and in some cases differences between groups may be statistically significant under one test, but not under another. LeVay, for example, notes that if the comparison between heterosexual and homosexual subjects is restricted to those who died of AIDS (thus eliminating any confounding influence of AIDS vs. non-AIDS deaths), then the statistical significance of the difference in nucleic volumes drops markedly (from $p < 0.001$ to $p < 0.028$). This difference between LeVay's own reanalysis and Hegarty's reanalysis discloses the essentially equivocal

nature of all statistical analysis. It is not one of the ambitions of this book to adjudicate on the appropriate statistical analysis for LeVay's data. However, I take LeVay's original analysis to indicate a division of some kind in the data. What LeVay's statistical test certifies is that the probability that two clusters in the INAH 3 data would emerge by chance (i.e., if subjects were assigned randomly to each category) is less than 1 in 1,000 ($p<0.001$). It seems substantially more likely, then, that something may differentiate the hypothalamic structures of these forty-one individuals into a dimorphic pattern. Other commentators seem also to concur about the reliability of LeVay's statistical analysis of this sample; for example, Suppe (1994) comments favorably on LeVay's statistical testing in a paper that is otherwise hostile to LeVay's study. The concerns of these commentators have been either that this is not a representative sample of the general population or that we are unable to infer specific functional differences from this anatomical difference.

14. For a meticulous reading of Sedgwick and Halley on this issue, see Deutscher (1997, chap. 1).

15. LeVay (1991) measured both the left and right INAH in fewer than half of his subjects: "In 15 cases the nuclei in both left and right hypothalami were traced. In 12 cases only the left hypothalamus was studied, and in 14 cases only the right" (1035). In a later text he comments, "As far as we know, the two members of each [nucleic] pair have the same structure, the same connections and the same function, so they are often casually referred to in the singular" (1993, 40).

4   Darwin's Nervous System

1. The Oxford English Dictionary lists these as obsolete meanings for reflex.

2. For example: "The sexual 'drive' in the human animal is . . . *originally detached* from what might otherwise be its natural foundation . . . Lacan always insisted upon Freud's terminological distinction whereby the drive is distinguished from the instinct precisely insofar as sexuality in the human animal is *intrinsically bound to representation*. This link between the drive and representation is what separates human sexuality from the natural function of instinct—not only in the occasional or 'perverse' instance, but in its very constitution" (Shepherdson, 2000, 86–87).

3. At medical school in Edinburgh, Darwin became friendly with one of his professors, the radical Lamarckian Robert Grant. Darwin spent his spare time with Grant collecting and classifying marine invertebrates. Through Grant, Darwin was introduced to Edinburgh's scientific and philosophical societies, and Grant's Lamarckism remained influential (in both positive and negative ways) on Darwin from that point on (Desmond and Moore 1991, 34–39). See *The Structure and Distribution of Coral Reefs* (1842), *A Monograph on the Subclass Cirripedia* (1851–54), *The Formation of Vegetable Mould, through the Action of Worms, with Observations on Their Habits* (1881) for Darwin's publications on (respectively) corals, barnacles. and worms. Rebecca Stott's (2003) popular account of the eight years Darwin spent dissecting barnacles before he wrote *The Origin of Species* elucidates the importance of these simple and lowly creatures to Darwin's thinking. See E. A. Wilson (2002) for some preliminary thoughts on the value of Darwin's barnacle research for feminism.

4. See Steele, Lindley, and Blanden (1998) for a recent attempt to argue for the plausibility of Lamarckism in contemporary scientific contexts.

5. Lamarck's theory of evolution is more complex than simply the mechanism of the inheritance of acquired characteristics. For Lamarck, evolution was due to two factors: (1) an innate tendency for organisms to evolve into higher and more complex structures (progressionism) and (2) the inheritance of acquired characteristics. Moreover, the innate capacity to

evolve was the primary motive force in evolution. The inheritance of acquired characteristics itself encompassed two kinds of modification: (1) modifications due to the direct effect of the environment (modifications that required no effort on behalf of the organism) and (2) modifications that arise due to the increased or decreased use of body parts; that is, disused organs and body parts atrophy and may even extinguish over time, whereas overused organs and body parts are built up. Furthermore, in a move that is precociously close to Mendel, Lamarck states that these ontogenetic changes are passed on to offspring only when two similarly modified individuals mate (modifications will be lost in the offspring of a modified and unmodified parent). See Elliot (1914) for an introduction to Lamarck's theory of evolution that is comprehensive and remains closely allied to Lamarck's original text.

6. This aspect of Darwinian evolution is argued at greater length in chapter 5.

7. *The Expression of the Emotions in Man and Animals* is not an account of the emotions per se, but rather an explanation of their instinctive bodily manifestation. For Darwin, it is emotions that cause bodily responses. It wasn't until 1884 and 1885 (respectively) that Lange and James published what became known as the James-Lange hypothesis, reversing this causal relation: "Bodily changes follow directly the perception of the exciting fact, and . . . our feeling of the same changes as they occur *is* the emotion . . . we feel sorry because we cry, angry because we strike, afraid because we tremble . . . Without the bodily states following on the perception, the latter would be purely cognitive in form, pale, colorless, destitute of emotional warmth. We might then see the bear, and judge it best to run, receive the insult and deem it right to strike, but we should not actually *feel* afraid or angry" (James 1890, 449–450). I am less interested in a theory of emotion per se than in how Darwin's theory of emotional expression illuminates neurophysiological matters.

5   Emotional Lizards

1. Sacks's interest in Freudian matters was established in his first book (1991; orig. pub. 1970), where he occasionally offers Freudian interpretations of neurological data. More recently (1998b), he has written about Freud's early neurological writings, and it is clear from interviews that he is well versed in Freud's work (http://www.oliversacks.com).

2. In this sense, Sacks reiterates the sentiment of Darwin's famous concluding sentence in the *Descent*: "We must acknowledge, as it seems to me, that man with all his noble qualities, with sympathy which feels for the most debased, with benevolence which extends not only to other men but to the humblest living creatures, with his god-like intellect which has penetrated into the movements and constitution of the solar system—with all these exalted powers—Man still bears in his bodily frame the indelible stamp of his lowly origin" (1871, 405).

3. To put this in specific theoretical terms, evolutionary systems approximate the movement of *différance*. It has been usual to see *différance* as a mechanism of signification; it is also a biological mechanism. That is, the identity of any biological entity (organism, organ, cell) is to be found in the movement of relationality—between individuals, within individuals over time, within groups, between organisms and their environment, among body parts, across cell membranes. Darwin made such an argument in relation to body parts (e.g., the eye) and to whole groups (species): "[Nature] can act on every internal organ, on every shade of constitutional difference, on the whole machinery of life" (1859, 69). It is clear from Darwin's texts and from his early notebooks that the aspect of Lamarckian evolution he most strongly rejected was that of progressionism: "the increasing complexity of organisation tending to form a regular gradation" (Lamarck 1809, 107). For Darwin, the character of any

organic being, and the character of nature itself, is generated by a system of biological differences (rather than through the unfolding of a blueprint of linear progress). This notion that identity is constituted through relationality is the mechanism that Derrida exploits under the name *différance*. Taking liberties with Derrida's celebrated deployment of Saussurian linguistics, I argue that "[a biological entity] is never present in and of itself, in a sufficient presence that would refer only to itself. Essentially, and lawfully, every [biological entity] is inscribed in a chain or in a system within which it refers to the other, to other [biological entities], by means of the systematic play of differences . . . In [biology], in the system of [biology], there are only differences" (Derrida 1982, 11). I have been attempting to highlight in Sacks's footnote the way he depicts human neurobiology as a play of biological differences not just within classes over vast periods of evolutionary time, but also between the classes mammalia and reptilia in the current epoch.

4. Myoclonus is the term for sudden, brief, involuntary movements of the muscles. Myoclonus is often a symptom in nervous system disorders like multiple sclerosis, Parkinson's disease, Alzheimer's disease, and Creutzfeldt-Jakob disease. Everyday examples of myoclonus include hiccups and jerks or "sleep starts" that some people experience while drifting off to sleep. Branchial myoclonus refers to the rhythmic twitching of the muscles of the face, palate, and/or throat.

5. The forebrain, or prosencephalon, is the "most anterior of the three expansions of the embryonic vertebrate brain" (Thain and Hickman 1996, 241). The thalamus and hypothalamus (diencephalon) and the cerebral hemispheres (telencephalon) arise from this embryonic structure. In evolutionary terms, these are the most recent structures in the mammalian brain. MacLean's triune model pertains only to these forebrain structures. The structures of the brainstem (i.e., the vertebrate mid brain, pons and medulla oblongata), which are thought to be concerned with aspects of vision and audition, reflex action, respiration, vascular and cardiac function, and proprioception, are not directly implicated in this model. MacLean argues that the vertebrate forebrain is essential for spontaneous, directed behavior and the tendency to explore. Experiments in the nineteenth century first demonstrated the specific effects of removal of the forebrain in vertebrates. Perhaps the most startling of these was observed in the frog; renarrating Goltz's experiments, the neurologist David Ferrier (1886) describes the effects of decerebration as follows: "Deprived of its cerebral hemispheres, the frog will maintain its normal attitude . . . If laid on its back, it will immediately turn on its face, and regain its station on its feet. If placed on a board, and the board tilted in any direction, the animal will make the appropriate bodily movement to throw its centre of gravity within the base of support. If its foot be pinched, it will hop away. If it is thrown in the water it will swim until it reaches the side of the vessel, and then clamber up and sit perfectly quiet. If its back be stroked gently, it will utter loud croaks . . . There is, so far, no difference between its behaviour and that of a frog in full possession of all its faculties. But yet a very remarkable difference is perceptible. The brainless frog, unless disturbed by any form of peripheral stimulus, will sit quiet in the same spot, and become converted to a mummy . . . surrounded by plenty it will die of starvation" (109–110).

6. This difference in emotional character is also effected by a difference in facial structure: fish, amphibians, and reptiles do not have the mobile facial structure necessary to support emotional expression. According to some theorists of emotion, this lack of facial mobility will prevent not just the expression of emotion, but its actual production; see, for example, the central role Silvan Tomkins (1962–1991) and Paul Ekman (1990) give to the face in the generation of emotion. Without a certain level of complexity in their facial musculature, emotional life (and its mammalian analogues: social bonding, play, and maternal care) is not possible.

7. E. O. Wilson's first book (1971) makes a similar claim in regard to ants, displacing the primacy hitherto given to worms: "Ants in fact are so abundant that they replace earthworms as the chief earth movers in the tropics . . . Recent research has shown they are nearly as important as earthworms in cold temperate forests as well" (1). Wilson's own work, as it emerged under the rubric of sociobiology (1975), was to become nearly as important as (and indeed, often replaces) Darwin's in contemporary commentaries on evolutionary theory.

8. Damasio's work (1994, 1999) on the neurology of emotion has achieved wider popular circulation than LeDoux's. However, Damasio seems more interested in rationality and consciousness than does LeDoux, which in the end tends to undermine the psychological potency of the affects in Damasio's work. Moreover, his theory of affect and self is neither as psychologically comprehensive nor as convincing as similar theories in infantile development and attachment studies (e.g., Beebe and Lachmann 1988; Fonagy 2000; Schore 1999; Stern 1985; Trevarthen 1998). I have chosen LeDoux's work as I think it highlights the issue of differentiated affects more usefully than does Damasio's. I am making no claim here that LeDoux's work is representative of contemporary neurobiological research on emotion; this nascent field encompasses a number of different conceptual orientations. An analysis of how these various researchers mobilize evolutionary theories in relation to the neurobiology of emotion would require an extended analysis of its own. My objective here is simply to open up a couple of avenues into this material for readers unfamiliar with the field.

9. Power and Dalgleish (1997) describe Schacter and Singer's 1962 study as "one of the classic top 10 psychological experiments" (79). Schacter and Singer injected 184 subjects with either epinephrine (adrenalin) or a saline placebo. The injection of epinephrine stimulated the sympathetic nervous system: subjects experienced this as palpitations, tremor, flushing, and accelerated breathing. Schacter and Singer found that the same state of physiological arousal was experienced as a different emotional state depending on the cognitive cues available to the subject: "Given a state of physiological arousal for which an individual has no immediate explanation, he will label this state and describe his feelings in terms of the cognitions available to him. To the extent that cognitive factors are potent determiners of emotional states, it should be anticipated that precisely the same state of physiological arousal could be labeled 'joy' or 'fury' or 'jealousy' or any of a great diversity of emotional states depending on the cognitive aspects of the situation" (398). Since the 1960s these appraisal theories of emotion have become massively influential ("Appraisal theory currently does not seem to have any serious rivals," Scherer 1999, 654), and they have become more sophisticated in approach (such that the difference between Darwinian/categorical theories and contemporary appraisal theories now requires careful delineation). See Scherer (1999) for an overview of appraisal theory and Scherer (1993) for an account of the relationship between appraisal theory and neuroscientific theories of emotion.

10. See, for example, the heated debate in the mainstream psychology literature in the 1980s about the relationship between cognition and affect (Lazarus, 1982, 1984; Zajonc 1980, 1984). Robert Zajonc disputed Richard Lazarus's claim that the affects are "postcognitive" (i.e., that they emerge only after basic cognitive processing, such as feature recognition, has been accomplished). Zajonc argued that affective reactions are not reliant on cognitive processing; they are primary, perhaps precognitive events: "It is entirely possible that the very first stage of the organism's reaction to stimuli and the very first element in retrieval are affective" (1980, 154).

11. LeDoux advocates a theory of basic, primary emotions, yet also integrates a mechanism of appraisal in the affects: "At the neural level, each emotional unit can be thought of as consisting of a set of inputs, an appraisal mechanism, and a set of outputs. The appraisal

mechanism is programmed by evolution to detect certain input or trigger stimuli that are relevant to the function of the network" (1996, 127). To my mind, any attempt to integrate an appraisal mechanism into the character of affects reintroduces a mechanism of cognitive processing. Appraisal is a mediating, low-level cogitating process ("to detect"); its introduction into the conceptual field undermines any claim to promote the primacy of the emotions (which are innately and directly triggered by particular stimuli). In this regard, LeDoux reinstalls the "cognitive monster" into the heart of his account of affect. His theory of affect would be conceptually stronger if it relied less on covert cognitive mechanisms and allied itself more faithfully with biological mechanisms.

12. See Robert Abelson (1963) for an early, and still underappreciated, argument for the importance of thinking about the interfaces of emotion and cognition: "There seems to have been no provision . . . for the study of cognition dealing with affect-laden objects—of 'hot cognition' as opposed to the 'cold cognition' of problem solving" (277).

•••••••• REFERENCES

••••••••

Abelson, Robert. 1963. Computer simulation of "hot" cognition. In *Computer simulation of personality: Frontier of psychological theory*, edited by Silvan S. Tomkins and Samuel Messick. New York: Wiley.

Alexander, Franz. 1934. The influence of psychologic factors upon gastro-intestinal disturbances: A symposium. 1. General principles, objectives, and preliminary results. *Psychoanalytic Quarterly* 3: 501–539.

Allen, Laura, Melissa Hines, James Shryne, and Roger Gorski. 1989. Two sexually dimorphic cell groups in the human brain. *Journal of Neuroscience* 9: 497–506.

American Psychiatric Association. 1994. *Diagnostic and statistical manual of mental disorders.* 4th ed. Washington, D.C.: American Psychiatric Association.

Angier, Natalie. 1999. *Woman: An intimate geography.* London: Virago.

Appenzeller, Otto, and Emilio Oribe. 1997. *The autonomic nervous system: An introduction to basic and clinical concepts.* 5th ed. Amsterdam: Elsevier.

Appignanesi, Lisa, and John Forrester. 1992. *Freud's women.* New York: Basic Books.

Bacon, Catherine. 1934. Typical personality trends and conflicts in cases of gastric disturbance. *Psychoanalytic Quarterly* 3: 540–557.

Bailey, Michael, and Richard Pillard. 1991. A genetic study of male sexual orientation. *Archives of General Psychiatry* 48: 1089–1096.

Barinaga, Marsha. 1991. Is homosexuality biological? *Science* 253: 956–957.

Barke, Megan, Rebecca Fribush, and Peter N. Stearns. 2000. Nervous breakdown in 20th-century American culture. *Journal of Social History* 33(3): 565–584.

Bayliss, William, and Ernest Starling. 1899. The movements and innervation of the small intestine. *Journal of Physiology* 24: 99–143.

Beard, George. 1895. *Sexual neurasthenia: Its hygiene, causes, symptoms and treatment.* New York: E. B. Trent.

Beebe, Beatrice, and Frank Lachmann. 1988. Mother-infant influence and precursors of psychic structure. In *Frontiers in self psychology*, edited by Arnold Goldberg. New York: Analytic Press.

Beer, Gillian. 1996a. Introduction. In Charles Darwin, *The origin of species*, edited by Gillian Beer. Oxford: Oxford University Press.

———. 1996b. *Open fields: Science in cultural encounter*. Oxford: Oxford University Press.

———. 2000. *Darwin's plots: Evolutionary narrative in Darwin, George Eliot and nineteenth century fiction*, 2nd ed. Cambridge, England: Cambridge University Press. (Orig. pub. 1983.)

Bemporad, Jules, and David Herzog, eds. 1989. *Psychoanalysis and eating disorders*. New York: Guilford.

Bernfeld, Siegfried. 1949. Freud's scientific beginnings. *American Imago* 6: 163–196.

———. 1951. Sigmund Freud, M.D., 1882–1885. *International Journal of Psychoanalysis* 32: 204–217.

Bernheimer, Charles, and Claire Kahane, eds. 1990. *In Dora's case: Freud—hysteria—feminism*. New York: Columbia University Press.

Bilder, Robert, and Frank LeFever, eds. 1998. *Neuroscience of the mind on the centennial of Freud's "Project for a scientific psychology."* (*Annals of the New York Academy of Sciences* 843). New York: New York Academy of Sciences.

Bowlby, John. 1947. *Forty-four juvenile thieves: Their characters and home-life*. London: Bailliere.

———. 1980. *Attachment and loss*, vol. 3: *Loss: Sadness and depression*. London: Hogarth.

Bowler, Peter. 1992. Lamarckism. In *Keywords in evolutionary biology*, edited by Evelyn Fox Keller and Elisabeth A. Lloyd. Cambridge, Mass.: Harvard University Press.

Breuer, Joseph, and Sigmund Freud. 1895. Studies on hysteria. In *The standard edition of the complete psychological works of Sigmund Freud*, vol. 2, edited by James Strachey. London: Hogarth, 1955.

Byne, William. 1995. Science and belief: Psychobiological research on sexual orientation. In *Sex, cells, and same-sex desire: The biology of sexual preference*, edited by John De Cecco and David Allen Parker. New York: Haworth.

Byne, William, Mitchell Lasco, Eileen Kemether, Akbar Shinwair, Mark Edgar, Susan Morgello, Liesl Jones, and Stuart Tobet. 2000. The interstitial nuclei of the human anterior hypothalamus: An investigation of sexual variation in volume and cell size, number and density. *Brain Research* 856: 254–258.

Cilliers, Paul. 1998. *Complexity and postmodernism: Understanding complex systems*. London: Routledge.

Clarke, Edwin, and L. S. Jacyna. 1987. *Nineteenth century origins of neuroscientific concepts*. Berkeley: University of California Press.

Copjec, Joan. 1987. Flavit et dissipati sunt. In *October: The first decade, 1976–1986*, edited by Annette Michelson, Rosalind Krauss, Douglas Krimp, and Joan Copjec. Cambridge, Mass.: MIT Press.

Curtis, Helena, and N. Sue Barnes. 1989. *Biology*, 5th ed. New York: Worth.

Damasio, Antonio. 1994. *Descartes' error: Emotion, reason, and the human brain*. New York: Avon.

———. 1997. Thinking and feeling. *Scientific American* June: 117–118.

———. 1999. *The feeling of what happens: Body and emotion in the making of consciousness*. New York: Harcourt Brace.

Darwin, Charles. 1842. The structure and distribution of coral reefs. In *The works of Charles Darwin*, vol. 7. New York: NYU Press, 1987.

———. 1851–1854. A monograph on the sub-class Cirripedia. Volume 1: The Lepadidae. In *The works of Charles Darwin*, vol. 11. New York: NYU Press.

———. 1859. *The origin of species*. Oxford: Oxford University Press, 1996.

———. 1871. *The descent of man and Selection in relation to sex*. Princeton: Princeton University Press, 1981.

———. 1872. *The expression of the emotions in man and animals*. Chicago: University of Chicago Press, 1965.

——. 1881. *The formation of vegetable mould, through the action of worms, with observations on their habits*. London: John Murray.

——. 1987. *Charles Darwin's notebooks, 1836–1844: Geology, transmutation of species, metaphysical enquiries*, edited by Paul H. Barrett, Peter J. Gautrey, Sandra Herbert, David Kohn, and Sydney Smith. Cambridge, England: Cambridge University Press.

David-Ménard, Monique. 1989. *Hysteria from Freud to Lacan: Body and language in psychoanalysis*, translated by Catherine Porter. Ithaca: Cornell University Press.

Dawkins, Richard. 1986. *The blind watchmaker*. Harlow, England: Longman.

De Cecco, John, and David Allen Parker. 1995. The biology of homosexuality: Sexual orientation or sexual preference? In *Sex, cells, and same-sex desire: The biology of sexual preference*, edited by John De Cecco and David Allen Parker. New York: Haworth.

Dennett, Daniel. 1995. *Darwin's dangerous idea: Evolution and the meanings of life*. Harmondsworth, England: Penguin.

Derrida, Jacques. 1978. Freud and the scene of writing. In *Writing and difference*, translated by Alan Bass. Chicago: University of Chicago Press.

——. 1982. Différance. In *Margins of philosophy*, translated by Alan Bass. Chicago: University of Chicago Press.

——. 1995. *Archive fever: A Freudian impression*, translated by Eric Prenowitz. Chicago: University of Chicago Press.

Desmond, Adrian, and James Moore. 1991. *Darwin*. Harmondsworth, England: Penguin.

Deutscher, Penelope. 1997. *Yielding gender: Feminism, deconstruction and the history of philosophy*. London: Routledge.

Didi-Huberman, Georges. 1982. *Invention of hysteria: Charcot and the photographic iconography of the Salpêtrière*, translated by Alisa Hartz. Cambridge, Mass.: MIT Press, 2003.

Doyle, Richard. 2003. *Wetwares: Experiments in post vital living*. Minneapolis: University of Minnesota Press.

Drossman, Douglas. 1999. The functional gastrointestinal disorders and the Rome II process. *Gut* 45 (supplement II): II1–II5.

Drossman, Douglas, F. H. Creed, K. W. Olden, J. Svedlund, B. B. Toner, and W. E. Whitehead. 1999. Psychosocial aspects of the functional gastrointestinal disorders. *Gut* 45 (supplement II): II25–II30.

Edelman, Gerald. 1992. *Bright air, brilliant fire*. Harmondsworth, England: Penguin.

Ekman, Paul. 1990. Voluntary facial action generates emotion-specific autonomic nervous system activity. *Psychophysiology* 27: 363–383.

Elfenbein, Debra, ed. 1995. *Living with Prozac and other selective serotonin reuptake inhibitors* (SSRIs): Personal accounts of life on antidepressants. San Francisco: Harper.

Elliot, Hugh. 1914. Introduction. In Jean Baptiste Lamarck, *Zoological philosophy*, translated by Hugh Elliot. London: Macmillan.

Ellis, Lee, and Linda Ebertz, eds. 1997. *Sexual orientation: Toward biological understanding*. Westport, Conn.: Praeger.

Fausto-Sterling, Anne. 1992. *Myths of gender: Biological theories about men and women*. Revised ed. New York: Basic Books.

——. 2000. *Sexing the body: Gender politics and the construction of sexuality*. New York: Basic Books.

Ferrier, David. 1886. *The functions of the brain*. 2d ed. London: Smith, Elder.

Fonagy, Peter. 2000. *Attachment theory and psychoanalysis*. New York: Other Press.

Fortun, Michael. 2003. *To speculate—on genomics*. Occasional paper, School for Social Science, Institute for Advanced Study. http://www.ss.ias.edu/home/papers.html.

Freud, Sigmund. 1878. Über Spinalganglien und Rückenmark des Petromyzon. *Sitzungsberichte der Akademie der Wissenschaften Wien (Mathematisch-Naturwissenschaftliche Klasse)* 3(78): 81–167.

———. 1886. Observation of a severe case of hemi-anaesthesia in a hysterical male. In *The standard edition of the complete psychological works of Sigmund Freud*, vol. 1, edited by James Strachey. London: Hogarth, 1966.

———. 1891. *On aphasia*, translated by E. Stengel. New York: International Universities Press.

———. 1893. Draft B: The aetiology of the neuroses. In *The standard edition of the complete psychological works of Sigmund Freud*, vol. 1, edited by James Strachey. London: Hogarth, 1966.

———. 1894a. Draft F: Collection III. In *The standard edition of the complete psychological works of Sigmund Freud*, vol. 1, edited by James Strachey. London: Hogarth, 1966.

———. 1894b. The neuro-psychoses of defence. In *The standard edition of the complete psychological works of Sigmund Freud*, vol. 3, edited by James Strachey. London: Hogarth, 1962.

———. 1895a. Draft G: Melancholia. In *The standard edition of the complete psychological works of Sigmund Freud*, vol. 1, edited by James Strachey. London: Hogarth, 1966.

———. 1895b. On the grounds for detaching a particular syndrome from neurasthenia under the description "anxiety neurosis." In *The standard edition of the complete psychological works of Sigmund Freud*, vol. 3, edited by James Strachey. London: Hogarth, 1962.

———. 1905. Fragment of an analysis of a case of hysteria. In *The standard edition of the complete psychological works of Sigmund Freud*, vol. 7, edited by James Strachey. London: Hogarth, 1953.

———. 1912. A discussion on masturbation. In *The standard edition of the complete psychological works of Sigmund Freud*, vol. 12, edited by James Strachey. London: Hogarth, 1958.

———. 1916. Introductory lectures on psycho-analysis (Lecture 24: The common neurotic state). In *The standard edition of the complete psychological works of Sigmund Freud*, vol. 16, edited by James Strachey. London: Hogarth, 1963.

———. 1918. From the history of an infantile neurosis. In *The standard edition of the complete psychological works of Sigmund Freud*, vol. 17, edited by James Strachey. London: Hogarth, 1955.

———. 1925a. An autobiographical study. In *The standard edition of the complete psychological works of Sigmund Freud*, vol. 20, edited by James Strachey. London: Hogarth, 1959.

———. 1925b. A note upon the "mystic writing pad." In *The standard edition of the complete psychological works of Sigmund Freud*, vol. 19, edited by James Strachey. London: Hogarth, 1961.

———. 1925c. The resistances to psychoanalysis. In *The standard edition of the complete psychological works of Sigmund Freud*, vol. 19, edited by James Strachey. London: Hogarth, 1961.

———. 2002. *The complete correspondence of Sigmund Freud and Karl Abraham, 1907–1925*, edited by Ernst Falzeder, translated by Caroline Schwarzacher. London: Karnac.

Furness, John Barton. 2000. Types of neurons in the enteric nervous system. *Journal of the Autonomic Nervous System* 81: 87–96.

Furness, John Barton, and Marcello Costa. 1987. *The enteric nervous system*. Edinburgh: Churchill Livingstone.

Gallagher, John. 1991. Hypothalamus study and coverage of it attract many barbs. *Advocate* October 8 (no. 587): 14–15.

Gallop, Jane. 1982. *The daughter's seduction: Feminism and psychoanalysis*. Ithaca: Cornell University Press.

Garber, Marjorie. 1995. *Vice versa: Bisexuality and the eroticism of everyday life*. New York: Simon and Schuster.

Gardiner, Judith Kegan. 1995. Can Ms. Prozac talk back? Feminism, drugs, and social constructionism. *Feminist Studies* 21: 501–517.

Gariepy, Cheryl. 2001. Intestinal motility disorders and the development of the enteric nervous system. *Pediatric Research* 49(5): 605–613.

Geerardyn, Filip. 1997. *Freud's project: The roots of psychoanalysis,* translated by Philippe Vandendaele. London: Rebus.

Gershon, Michael, D. 1998. *The second brain.* New York: Harper-Perennial.

———. 1999. The enteric nervous system: A second brain. *Hospital Practice* July 15: 31–52.

Gessen, Masha, and David McGowan. 1992. Raiders of the gay gene. *Advocate* March 24 (no. 599): 60–62.

Goleman, Daniel. 1995. *Emotional intelligence.* New York: Bantam.

Goodall, Jane. 1996. General adaptation syndrome: Hypochondrias of the fin de siècle. In *Aesthesia and the economy of the senses,* edited by Helen Grace. Kingswood, Australia: PAD.

Gordo-López, Angel, and Richard Cleminson. 1999. Queer science/queer psychology: A biosocial inoculation project. *Theory and Psychology* 9(2): 282–288.

Gorski, Roger, J. H. Gordon, J. E. Shryne, and A. M. Southam. 1978. Evidence for a morphological sex difference within the medial preoptic area of the rat brain. *Brain Research* 148: 333–346.

Gosling, Francis. 1987. *Before Freud: Neurasthenia and the American medical community 1870–1910.* Urbana: University of Illinois Press.

Goyal, Raj, and Ikuo Hirano. 1996. Mechanisms of disease: The enteric nervous system. *New England Journal of Medicine* 334(17): 1106–1115.

Greenfield, Susan. 2000. *The private life of the brain.* Harmondsworth, England: Penguin.

Griggers, Camilla. 1997. *Becoming-woman.* Minneapolis: University of Minnesota Press.

Grosz, Elizabeth. 1989. *Sexual subversions: Three French feminists.* Sydney: Allen and Unwin.

———. 1999. Darwin and feminism: Preliminary investigations for a possible alliance. *Australian Feminist Studies* 14(29): 31–45.

Guttmann, Giselher, and Inge Scholz-Strasser, eds. 1999. *Freud and the neurosciences: From brain research to the unconscious.* Vienna: Austrian Academy of Sciences.

Halley, Janet. 1994. Sexual orientation and the politics of biology: A critique of the argument from immutability. *Stanford Law Review* 46: 503–568.

Hamer, Dean, Stella Hu, Victoria Magnuson, Nan Hu, and Angela Pattatuci. 1993. A linkage between DNA markers on the X chromosome and male sexual orientation. *Science* 261: 321–327.

Haraway, Donna. 1989. *Primate visions.* New York: Routledge.

Hegarty, Peter. 1997. Materializing the hypothalamus: A performative account of the "gay brain." *Feminism and Psychology* 7(3): 355–372.

Hewitt, John P., Michael R. Fraser, and Leslie Beth Berger. 2000. Is it me or is it Prozac? Antidepressants and the construction of the self. In *Pathology and the postmodern: Mental illness as discourse and experience,* edited by Dwight Fee. London: Sage.

Hofman, Michel, and Dick Swaab. 1989. The sexually dimorphic nucleus of the preoptic area in the human brain: A comparative morphometric study. *Journal of Anatomy* 164: 55–72.

Hrdy, Sarah. 1981. *The woman that never evolved.* Cambridge, Mass.: Harvard University Press.

———. 2000. *Mother nature: Natural selection and the female of the species.* London: Vintage.

Hunter, Diane. 1985. Hysteria, psychoanalysis, and feminism: The case of Anna O. In *The (m)other tongue: Essays in feminist psychoanalytic interpretation,* edited by Shirley Nelson Garner, Claire Kahane, and Madelon Sprengnether. Ithaca: Cornell University Press.

Irigaray, Luce. 1985. *Speculum of the other woman,* translated by Gillian Gill. Ithaca: Cornell University Press.

James, William. 1890. *Principles of psychology*, vol. 2. London: Dover.

Jones, J., J. Boorman, P. Cann, A. Forbes, J. Gomborone, K. Heaton, P. Hungin, D. Kumar, G. Libby, R. Spiller, N. Read, D. Silk, and P. Whorwell. 2000. British Society of Gastroenterology guidelines for the management of the irritable bowel syndrome. *Gut* 47 (supplement II): II1–II19.

Kaplan-Solms, Karen, and Mark Solms. 2000. *Clinical studies in neuropsychoanalysis: Introduction to a depth neuropsychology*. London: Karnac.

Kim, Doe-Young, and Michael Camilleri. 2000. Serotonin: A mediator of brain-gut connection. *American Journal of Gastroenterology* 95(10): 2698–2709.

Kirby, Vicki. 1997. *Telling flesh: The substance of the corporeal*. New York: Routledge.

Kramer, Peter. 1993. *Listening to Prozac*. New York: Penguin.

———. 1997a. Afterword. In *Listening to Prozac*. New York: Penguin.

———. 1997b. *Should you leave?* New York: Scribner.

Lamarck, Jean Baptiste. 1809. *Zoological philosophy*, translated by Hugh Elliot. Chicago: University of Chicago Press, 1984.

Lane, Christopher. 1994. Philosophy of the unconscious: Vacillating on the scene of writing in Freud's "Project." *Prose Studies* 17(2): 98–129.

Langley, John. 1921. *Autonomic nervous system*. Cambridge, England: Heffer.

Laplanche, Jean, and Jean-Bertrand Pontalis. 1988. *The language of psychoanalysis*. London: Karnac.

Lazarus, R. 1982. Thoughts on the relation between cognition and emotion. *American Psychologist* 37(9): 1019–1024.

———. 1984. On the primacy of cognition. *American Psychologist* 39(2): 124–129.

LeDoux, Joseph. 1996. *Emotional brain: The mysterious underpinnings of emotional life*. New York: Simon and Schuster.

LeVay, Simon. 1991. A difference in hypothalamic structure between heterosexual and homosexual men. *Science* 253: 1034–1037.

———. 1993. *The sexual brain*. Cambridge, Mass: MIT Press.

———. 1996. *Queer science: The use and abuse of research into homosexuality*. Cambridge, Mass.: MIT Press.

———. 1997. *Albrick's gold*. London: Hodder Headline.

LeVay, Simon, and Dean Hamer. 1994. Evidence for a biological influence in male homosexuality. *Scientific American* 270: 44–49.

Levey, Harry. 1934. Oral trends and oral conflicts in a case of duodenal ulcer. *Psychoanalytic Quarterly* 3: 574–582.

Levine, Maurice. 1934. Pregenital trends in a case of chronic diarrhoea and vomiting. *Psychoanalytic Quarterly* 3: 583–588.

Lorenz, Konrad. 1965. Introduction. In Charles Darwin, *The expression of the emotions in man and animals*. Chicago: University of Chicago Press.

Lundgren, O. 2000. Sympathetic input into the enteric nervous system. *Gut* 47 (supplement IV): IV33–IV35.

MacLean, Paul. 1990. *The triune brain: Role in paleocerebral functions*. New York: Plenum.

Maddox, John. 1991. Is homosexuality hard-wired? *Nature* 353(6339): 13.

Martin, Paul. 1997. *The sickening mind: Brain, behavior, immunity and disease*. London: Harper Collins.

Masserman, Jules. 1941. Psychodynamisms in anorexia nervosa and neurotic vomiting. *Psychoanalytic Quarterly* 10: 211–242.

Metzl, Jonathan. 2001. Prozac and the pharmacokinetics of narrative form. *Signs: Journal of Women in Culture and Society* 27(2): 347–380.

Miller, Laurence. 1991. *Freud's brain: Neuropsychodynamic foundations of psychoanalysis*. New York: Guilford.

Miller, S. 2000. Control of peripheral sympathetic prevertebral ganglion neurones by colonic mechanosensory afferents. *Gut* 47 (supplement IV): IV28–IV29.

Mitchell, Stephen, and Lewis Aron, eds. 1999. *Relational psychoanalysis: The emergence of a tradition*. New York: Analytic Press.

Morgan, Elaine. 1997. *The descent of woman*. Revised ed. London: Souvenir Press. (Orig. pub. 1972.)

Murphy, Timothy. 1997. *Gay science: The ethics of sexual orientation research*. New York: Columbia University Press.

Nierenberg, Ona. 1998. A hunger for science: Psychoanalysis and the "gay gene." *differences: A Journal of Feminist Cultural Studies* 10(1): 209–242.

Panksepp, Jaak. 1998. *Affective neuroscience: The foundations of human and animal emotions*. New York: Oxford University Press.

Phillips, Adam. 1999. *Darwin's worms*. London: Faber and Faber.

Power, Mick, and Tim Dalgleish. 1997. *Cognition and emotion: From order to disorder*. Hove, England: Psychology Press.

Powley, T. L. 2000. Vagal input to the enteric nervous system. *Gut* 47 (supplement IV): IV30–IV32.

Pribram, Karl H., and Merton M. Gill. 1976. *Freud's "Project" reassessed*. London: Hutchinson.

Rahman, Qazi, and Ken Silber. 2000. Sexual orientation and the sleep-wake cycle: A preliminary investigation. *Archives of Sexual Behavior* 29(2): 127–134.

Rahman, Qazi, and Glenn Wilson. 2003. Born gay? The psychobiology of human sexual orientation. *Personality and Individual Differences* 34(8): 1337–1382.

Ramachandran , V. S., and Sandra Blakeslee. 1998. *Phantoms in the brain*. New York: William Morrow.

Rosario, Vernon. 1997. Homosexual bio-histories: Genetic nostalgias and the quest for paternity. In *Science and homosexualities*, edited by Vernon Rosario. New York: Routledge.

Rudin, Norah. 1997. *Dictionary of modern biology*. Hauppauge, N.Y.: Baron's.

Sacks, Oliver. 1991. *Migraine*. Revised ed. Sydney: Picador. (Orig. pub. 1970.)

——. 1995. *An anthropologist on Mars*. Sydney: Picador.

——. 1996. *Island of the colour-blind*. Sydney: Picador.

——. 1998a. Origins of genius: Freud's early years. *DoubleTake* 4(4): 119–126.

——. 1998b. The other road: Freud as neurologist. In *Freud: Conflict and culture*, edited by Michael S. Roth. New York: Knopf.

Schacter, Stanley, and Jerome Singer. 1962. Cognitive, social, and physiological determinants of emotional state. *Psychological Review* 69: 379–399.

Scherer, Klaus. 1993. Neuroscience projections to current debates in emotion psychology. *Cognition and Emotion* 7(1): 1–41.

——. 1999. Appraisal theory. In *Handbook of cognition and emotion*, edited Tim Dalgleish and Mick Power. Chichester, England: Wiley.

Schore, Alan. 1999. *Affect regulation and the origin of the self: The neurobiology of emotional development*. Hillsdale, N.J.: Lawrence Erlbaum.

Sedgwick, Eve Kosofsky. 1990. *Epistemology of the closet*. Berkeley: University of California Press.

——. 1993. Queer and now. In *Tendencies*. Durham, N.C.: Duke University Press.

Sedgwick, Eve Kosofsky, and Adam Frank. 1995. Shame in the cybernetic fold: Reading Silvan Tomkins. In *Shame and its sisters: A Silvan Tomkins reader*, edited by Eve Kosofsky Sedgwick and Adam Frank. Durham, N.C.: Duke University Press.

Shepherdson, Charles. 2000. *Vital signs: Nature, culture, psychoanalysis*. New York: Routledge.

Showalter, Elaine. 1985. *The female malady: Women, madness, and English culture (1830–1980)*. New York: Pantheon.

———. 1997. *Hystories: Hysterical epidemics and modern media*. New York: Columbia University Press.

Slater, Lauren. 1998. *Prozac diary*. New York: Random House.

Slimp, Jefferson, Benjamin Hart, and Robert Goy. 1978. Heterosexual, autosexual and social behavior of adult male rhesus monkeys with medial preoptic-anterior hypothalamus lesions. *Brain Research* 142: 105–122.

Solms, Mark, and Michael Saling, eds. and trans. 1990. *A moment of transition: Two neuroscientific articles by Sigmund Freud*. London: Karnac.

Solomon, Andrew. 1998. Anatomy of melancholy. *New Yorker* January 12: 46–61.

———. 2001. *The noonday demon: An atlas of depression*. New York: Simon and Schuster.

Steele, Edward, Robyn Lindley, and Robert Blanden. 1998. *Lamarck's signature: How retrogenes are changing Darwin's natural selection paradigm*. Sydney: Allen and Unwin.

Stein, Edward. 1993. Evidence for queer genes: An interview with Richard Pillard. *GLQ: A Journal of Lesbian and Gay Studies* 1(1): 93–110.

———. 1999. *The mismeasure of desire: The science, theory and ethics of sexual orientation*. Oxford: Oxford University Press.

Stern, Daniel. 1985. *The interpersonal world of the infant*. New York: Basic Books.

Stott, Rebecca. 2003. *Darwin and the barnacle*. London: Faber and Faber.

Suppe, Frederick. 1994. Explaining homosexuality: Philosophical issues, and who cares anyhow? *Journal of Homosexuality* 27(3/4): 223–268.

Swaab, Dick, Wilson Chung, Frank Kruijver, Michel Hofman, and Tatjana Ishunina. 2001. Structural and functional sex differences in the human hypothalamus. *Hormones and Behavior* 40: 93–98.

Swaab, Dick, and E. Fliers. 1985. A sexually dimorphic nucleus in the human brain. *Science* 228: 1112–1115.

Swaab, Dick, L. Gooren, and Michel Hofman. 1992. The human hypothalamus in relation to gender and sexual orientation. *Progress in Brain Research* 93: 205–219.

Swaab, Dick, and Michel Hofman. 1995. Sexual differentiation of the human hypothalamus in relation to gender and sexual orientation. *Trends in Neuroscience* 18(6): 264–270.

Swaab, Dick, Jiang-Ning Zhou, Mariann Fodor, and Michel Hofman. 1997. Sexual differentiation of the human hypothalamus: Differences according to sex, sexual orientation, and transsexuality. In *Sexual orientation: Toward biological understanding*, edited by Lee Ellis and Linda Ebertz. Westport, Conn.: Praeger.

Talley, Nicholas. 2001. Serotonergic neuroenteric modulators. *Lancet* 358: 2061–2068.

Terry, Jennifer. 2000. "Unnatural acts" in nature: The scientific fascination with queer animals. *GLQ: A Journal of Lesbian and Gay Studies* 6(2): 151–193.

Thain, Michael, and Michael Hickman. 1996. *Dictionary of biology*. Harmondsworth, England: Penguin.

Tomkins, Silvan S. 1962–1991. *Affect, imagery, consciousness*. Vols. 1–4. New York: Springer.

Trevarthen, Colwyn. 1998. The concept and foundations of infant intersubjectivity. In *Intersubjective communication and emotion in early ontogeny*, edited by Stein Braten. Cambridge, England: Cambridge University Press.

Walton, Jean. 2002. Female peristalsis. *differences: A Journal of Feminist Cultural Studies* 13(2): 57–89.

Wilhelmsen, Ingvard. 2000. Brain-gut axis as an example of the bio-psycho-social model. *Gut* 47 (supplement IV): IV5–IV7.

Wilson, Edward O. 1971. *The insect societies*. Cambridge, Mass.: Belknap Press of Harvard University Press.

——. 1975. *Sociobiology: The new synthesis*. Cambridge, Mass.: Belknap Press of Harvard University Press.

Wilson, Elizabeth A. 1996. Projects for a scientific psychology: Freud, Derrida and connectionist theories of cognition. *differences: A Journal of Feminist Cultural Studies* 8(3): 21–52.

——. 1998. *Neural geographies: Feminism and the microstructure of cognition*. New York: Routledge.

——. 2002. Biologically inspired feminism: Response to Helen Keane and Marsha Rosengarten, "On the Biology of Sexed Subjects." *Australian Feminist Studies* 17(39): 283–285.

Wilson, George. 1934. Typical personality trends and conflicts in cases of spastic colitis. *Psychoanalytic Quarterly* 3: 558–573.

Woods, Jackie, D. H. Alpers, and P. L. R. Andrews. 1999. Fundamentals of neurogastroenterology. *Gut* 45 (supplement II): II6–II16.

Wurtzel, Elizabeth. 1995. *Prozac nation: Young and depressed in America*. New York: Riverhead.

Zajonc, Robert. 1980. Feeling and thinking: Preferences need no inferences. *American Psychologist* 35(2): 151–175.

——. 1984. On the primacy of affect. *American Psychologist* 39(2): 117–123.

Zita, Jacqueline N. 1998. *Body talk: Philosophical reflections on sex and gender*. New York: Columbia University Press.

········

Expression of the Emotions in Man and Animals (Darwin), 63–77; principle of antithesis, 70; principle of direct action of the nervous system, 71–74; principle of serviceable associated habits, 70

Feminism: antibiologism in, 1–14, 98 n.1; body and, 1–14, 82–83: evolution and, 64, 82–83, 87–88, 90–91, 94–95, 98 n.1
Formation of Vegetable Mould, Through the Action of Worms, with Observations on their Habits (Darwin), 89–91, 108 n.3
Fortun, Michael, 58–9
Frau Emmy von N. (Freud's patient), 4, 31–34, 42–43, 45, 47, 100 n.1
Freud, Sigmund, 1–14, 15–29, 31–34, 42–43, 45, 47, 68, 80, 91; biological reductionism in, 3, 11–13, 22; Breuer, Joseph and, 2, 4–5, 9–11, 31–32, 100 nn.1–2; classification of the neuroses, 17; critique of neurological localizationism, 20; fish and, 2–3; Lamarck and, 68; theory of conversion hysteria, 1, 7; theory of neurasthenia, 17, 22, 25
Functional Gastrointestinal Disorders (FGIDs). *See* Irritable bowel syndrome (IBS)

Gastric symptomology, 4, 32–33, 35, 37–47, 104 n.17, 104 n.19
Gershon, Michael, 34–36, 41–44, 102 n.6
Greenfield, Susan, 86
Griggers, Camilla, 24, 27–28, 100 n.8
Gut, 31–47; brain and, 37, 40, 42; depression and, 38, 43–47, 104 n.19; Emmy von N., 32–33, 42–43; functional vs. organic disorders, 38–43; lumen, 44; neurogastroenterology of, 34–43; of dog, 101 n.5; of Hydra, 44, 46; of worm, 44, 89–90; psychoanalysis and, 33–34, 38, 42–47; psychology of, 32–47, 104 n.19; serotonin and, 36, 39. *See also* Nervous system: vagus nerves

Homosexuality, neurological theories of, 49–53, 61–62, 105 n.2, 106 n.8, 107 n.11. *See also* LeVay, Simon
Hypnosis, 2, 31–33, 47
Hysteria, 1–14, 31–33; biology of, 4–5, 8, 10, 11–13; case histories, 4; conversion hysteria, 4–13, 22, 100 n.2; etiology, 2, 9, 11, 17, 39, 100 n.2; feminism and, 3, 4; ideation and, 5, 33, 44–45, 104 n.19; male, 12–13; somatization disorder, 38, 103 n.10. *See also* Augustine; Elisabeth von R.; Frau Emmy von N.; Louise K.

Interstitial nuclei of the anterior hypothalamus (INAH), 52–56, 61, 106 n.8, 107 nn.10–11, 107 n.13. *See also* LeVay, Simon; Nervous system: hypothalamus
Irritable bowel syndrome (IBS), 36–39, 103 n.11

Kirby, Vicki, 7–8, 98 n.10
Kramer, Peter, 15–16, 23–29, 98 n.1; Freud and, 16, 27–28; kindling model of depression, 24–26, 29, 99 n.7

Lamarck, Jean Baptiste, 65–70, 76, 108 n.5. *See also* Evolution: inheritance of acquired characteristics
Lamprey, 1–3
LeDoux, Joseph, 3, 83–95, 103 n.14, 111 n.8, 111 n.11
LeVay, Simon, 3, 49–62, 105 n.3; critical responses to, 49–50, 54–56, 59, 106 n.4, 107 n.13; details of 1991 study, 51–53; dimorphic vs. divergent patterns in data, 51–59. *See also* Reticulation
Listening to Prozac (Kramer), 15–16, 24–29; critical responses to, 15, 27–28, 98 n.1, 100 n.8, 100 n.12
Lorenz, Konrad, 69
Louise K. (Stekel's patient), 105 n.19
Lucy (Kramer's patient), 4, 15, 23, 25

MacLean, Paul, 3, 84–87, 90, 92, 94–95, 110 n.5
Melancholia, 17, 20, 22–23, 38, 45, 100 n.2

Nervous system: autonomic nervous system (ANS), 35, 73, 75, 76, 101 n.4; brain-gut axis, 40–41; central nervous system (CNS), 34–38, 40–42, 44–45, 47, 101 n.4; cortex, 6, 10, 18–20, 22, 37, 60–61, 86, 95, 97 n.5; dimorphism, 50–59, 61, 107 n.12; emotion and, 64, 70–71, 84, 91–94, 103 n.14, 104 n.17; enteric nervous system (ENS), 33–47, 73, 101 n.4; Freud and, 18–21, 97 n.2; habit and, 71–74; hierarchy, 27, 43, 84, 86; hypothalamus, 51–54, 59–62, 105 n.1, 106 n.8, 107 n.11, 108 n.15, 110 n.5; in dog, 101 n.5; in fish, 2; in frog, 63–64, 71, 75, 77, 110 n.5; in lower animals, 1–3, 64, 82, 92, 95; libidinized, 18–22; limbic system, 84–86, 93–95; mammalian, 59, 82, 85–87, 95; parasympathetic branch, 35, 60, 73–74, 101 n.4; peripheral nervous system, 10, 13, 21, 34, 63–65, 101 n.4; reflex, 12, 18–22, 63–64, 71–73, 77, 101 n.4, 110 n.5; relation between CNS and ENS, 35–37, 40–45; reptilian, 79–86, 92–95; sexuality and, 49–51, 54–57, 61–62, 106 n.5; sympathetic branch, 35, 60, 73, 75, 77, 101 n.4, 111 n.9; vagus nerves, 36, 42–43, 102 n.8

Nervous weakness. *See* Neurasthenia

Neurasthenia, 16–19, 22, 37, 99 nn.2–3; etiology, 17–23; male vs. female, 17–18, 21–22; masturbation and, 17, 19–21; neurasthenic melancholia, 20–21

Neurological determinism, 16, 20, 23, 26–29

Origin of Species (Darwin), 65, 88–89, 108 n.3

Phantom limbs, 98

Prozac, 15, 26

Psychoanalysis: body and, 1–4, 7–13, 18–19, 42, 98 n.8, 104 n.19; inheritance of acquired characteristics and, 68; neuro-science and, 44, 97 n.5; scientific beginnings, 1–2

Reticulation, 51, 56–59, 106 n.6

Sacks, Oliver, 2–3, 79–87, 90, 94, 98 n.7; Freud and, 109 n.1

Salpêtrière, 5, 12

Schacter, Stanley and Jerome Singer, 92, 111 n.9

Sedgwick, Eve Kosofsky, 57; Adam Frank and, 58, 83, 92, 93

Serotonin and SSRIs, 15–16, 26, 28, 36, 39–41, 43, 45, 47, 102 n.7, 103 n.11

Showalter, Elaine, 5–8, 24, 98 n.6

Solomon, Andrew, 46–47

Somatic compliance. *See* Hysteria: biology of

Strachey, James, 2, 12, 103 n.9

Stress, 7, 24, 34, 39, 40, 99 n.7

Sympathy, organic, 73–74, 77

Tomkins, Silvan, 83, 110 n.6

Transference, 34, 38, 42–44, 46–47, 103 n.11, 104 n.16

Triune brain, 84–87, 110 n.5

Vomiting, 36, 39, 46, 74, 102 n.7, 104 n.19

Worms, 44, 65–66, 70, 89–90, 94, 108 n.3, 111 n.7

Elizabeth A. Wilson is an Australian Research Council Research Fellow at the Research Institute for the Humanities and Social Sciences, University of Sydney. She is the author of *Neural Geographies: Feminism and the Microstructure of Cognition* (Routledge, 1998).

Library of Congress Cataloging-in-Publication Data
Wilson, Elizabeth A. (Elizabeth Ann)
Psychosomatic : feminism and the neurological body /
Elizabeth A. Wilson.
Includes bibliographical references and index.
ISBN 0-8223-3356-2 (cloth : alk. paper)
ISBN 0-8223-3365-1 (pbk. : alk. paper)
1. Sex differences. 2. Neurosciences. 3. Feminist theory.
4. Neuropsychology.
I. Title.
QP81.5W557 2004   305.42′01—dc22   2004001307